that look

that look

A Child of Sexual Abuse Remembers

KAY FRASER

Published 2024
by Kay Fraser

ISBN 978-0-473-72493-1

© Copyright Kay Fraser 2024

All rights reserved.

Except for the purpose of fair reviewing, no part of this publication may be reproduced or transmitted in any form or by any means, electronic or mechanical, including photocopying, recording or any information storage and retrieval system, without prior written permission from the publisher.

COPYPRESS

Designed and distributed in New Zealand by CopyPress,
Nelson, New Zealand. www.copypress.co.nz

For my lady judge who told me:

"The courts are full of cases of child sexual abuse within families, but these cases are not being reported or talked about."

Contents

Introduction	1
In the Beginning	6
A Revelation	32
Talks With My Mother	46
Paris and Writing	56
Tapping into the Past	71
More to Learn	93
Writing the Screenplay	101
Inside My Psyche	111
Strange Thoughts from Hobart	137
Final Revelations – at Home	149
On Memory	158

All names used are fictional.

Introduction

A winter's day in Auckland, New Zealand and rain begins to fall. It was to be a life-defining day for me.

There was a party underway – the usual Saturday afternoon get-together for these neighbours in their early thirties. The adults, mostly parents, were drinking their home-made brew under the house while their children, between the ages of two to seven years old, were in a room next door, sitting amongst cushions scattered around the floor. The children were waiting for a record to be played and they were excited. It was 1950 and this was a new recording they had not heard before. There was great anticipation. Among the eight or nine children there was one little girl, around five years old, who sat quietly off to one side. She appeared contained and not at all excited like the other children.

One of the parents placed the record on the turntable and a deep male voice began to tell the children about the snow goose who had a gunshot wound to her wing and was unable to fly. Also in the story, there was Philip, a disabled man who lived alone in a lighthouse on the coast of Essex in England, and Fritha, a shy young girl from a local village. This was Paul Gallico's tale, *The Snow Goose*.

The calm, strong voice echoing round the room calmed the children and silence reigned. The story begins with the girl-child arriving at the home of Philip with the hurt snow goose in her arms. He had a reputation as a healer, and she hoped he would be able to heal the bird she had picked up from the shore. Although almost afraid of the man, Fritha's desire to have the bird fly again ensured she maintained contact with Philip over the next few months.

It was at this early stage in the story that the little girl sitting by herself became spellbound by what she was hearing. The deep voice went on to explain how Philip sailed in his boat from the marshlands of Essex to Dunkirk to help the men fleeing the shores of Northern France during the Second World War. Yet this was not the part of the story the girl was captivated by. It was as the bird slowly healed and began to make tentative flights which enthralled the listening child. She was almost mesmerised by the story. Eventually, when the snow goose flew high into the sky, her eyes glistened in delight.

When the recording ended the children jumped up ready to play outside. The rain had stopped, and while the parents drank on, play beckoned and the recording was forgotten. The children ran outside with one exception – the little girl who had listened so intently. She raised herself slowly from the floor and, deep in thought, walked quietly across the road, back to her home. All this child wanted to do was to be alone with her thoughts. The story had been one of rejuvenation and hope and of better things to come. Instinctively she had understood this. The story had given her a window into the possibilities of another life – one not all bad, and not so difficult. I know because I was that little girl.

This memory came back to me as I began to write my mother's story. I was almost seventy years old and had no idea why I should suddenly remember listening to this delightful tale. It was not part of my mother's story, and at the time I did not see any reason why I should conjure up the image of a hurt bird who is healed and able to fly again. What I also did not know was this story would sustain me in these latter years of my life as I recalled the happenings within my family.

I did know there was a story to write. I assumed it was about my mother because I found her long journey into religion very interesting. Her deep spirituality suggested to me her story was inspiring and it could possibly help others who were on a similar path – I thought. Little did I know it was *my* story that needed to be told. I had led an interesting life but nothing of note to write about – I thought. If I had known where I was heading would I have begun to write? The answer is a resounding no. Yet it was a long time and some way into my writing before I understood the full significance of what I was attempting to write about.

Writing projects have always interested me. As a schoolgirl, it was my favourite occupation. Then, after a business career in London revolving round the early days of the computer industry, I went back to university in Sydney as a forty-something woman. Studying for a BA and then a PhD was a challenging and stimulating time for me; I was in my element. History was the subject I fell in love with and spent many hours researching for and writing essays. It was the ideal background for my big project (not that I knew there was a big project on my horizon). I have always asked a lot of questions. A good trait to have when studying history. After finishing my studies, I wrote a couple of history-based books and then turned to my mother for her story.

Now, as I begin to write my story, I realise that I began this narrative almost thirty years ago and it did not begin with my mother. The thesis I chose to do for my honours year at Sydney University was about working women in the English working class and this was the subject I carried on with for my PhD. At the time I did wonder why I had chosen this topic. It seemed quite out of character considering my interests and the rather worldly woman I had become. An issue more concerned with the rise of the middle class or perhaps an analysis of feminism and what it meant for women generally would seem more in keeping with my outward persona.

One day, as I walked home along a tree-lined laneway edging Sydney Harbour, I had one of those knowing moments. It was a university day and I had been in the library for a few hours reading up, no doubt, on the working class. The gentle lapping of the sea and the birds chattering in the trees filled me with a calmness. Suddenly it came to me. My father was from the working-class mould and my choice of subject was an attempt to understand him.

The outstanding issue I remember learning about in connection with my father was the importance to a man from this background of his role as the provider to his family. This was a significant part of what it meant to be a man in the working class. My father excelled in this role. At the time I did not give much thought to why I wanted to understand my father although it felt relevant to have recognised the connection.

When I began to write about my mother it was a similar process. I did not consider I was looking to understand her in relation to myself. It was more out of an admiration for her many religious experiences which made me want to explore her life and thoughts.

As a young woman of thirty-eight years old, my mother, Peggy, began her journey through a diverse number of groups which were all connected to religious or self-help organisations. She did an enormous amount of reading and practice within various prayer or meditation groups over a period of fifty-five years. I was proud of what I saw as an independent, free-thinking individual who just happened to be my mother.

I had no idea of what really lay beneath the quest to tell her story. I was not looking for understanding and information about our family. What sparked my interest was the fact my mother's story ended, as a ninety-four-year-old, where she had begun – in the Christian religion.

I did not wonder what exactly she had been doing journeying through all the different organisations or even how she had changed over time. Or, whether she had learnt anything personal from her journey. These questions were not my concern. What did interest me is why after all her journeying, did she turn back to Christianity? What was it about the Christian church that was able to hold her in such sway? It was this issue, and only this issue, about my mother which worried away at me for a long time.

My apparent lack of interest in any personal interaction with my mother suggests an intellectual search for understanding. It was much more than that. The writing of her experiences within religion and her return to the Christian church was pivotal to helping me uncover my own personal story. Not that I knew this at the time. I look back now and wonder why it all happened the way it did.

The way my story unfolded is worthy of note. Gradually over a decade, memories emerged from deep inside me. Sometimes remembering came about because of particular words, an action, a painting, or a flying bird. Always, well most times, I was able to handle what was revealed. If it had all come at the same time, I think I would have been overwhelmed. Someone, something was looking after me.

Underlying this account of my life, there is a theme of how we remember only when we are willing and able. When we do recapture memories in this way they arrive surely and distinctly. There are no doubts.

Carl Jung's words explain what was involved for me. He wrote, 'Until you make the unconscious conscious, it will direct your life and you will call it fate.' Looking at my life and the way I have lived it and what I have experienced, I can see so very clearly how deep within me the unconscious has ruled supreme for virtually seventy years.

In the Beginning

My parents came from quite different backgrounds. More than simply being from the working class my father was brought up in a family that lived on the wrong side of the tracks. He knew poverty and social disadvantage as a boy. I think he got himself into all sorts of childhood mischief. My mother, on the other hand, was from a more genteel family. Throughout her life, Peggy loved to say she was from missionary stock. Well, she was, from a long time ago. They were an attractive couple. He with his rugged good looks and my mother with her fine figure and healthy appearance.

During the war, she became a model for the pictorial magazine *Pix* in New Zealand: a photograph I still have shows her in a bathing suit waving a swimming cap. She looks so innocent and is obviously in excellent fettle. It was this picture which went off with others as a distraction for the servicemen during the Second World War.

Part of what made my father so attractive to Peggy was his personality. He was very outgoing and loved music and dancing. There was a definite charisma about him. My mother was more introverted. They were apparently deeply in love and were married just before my father went off to war. One of my mother's friends told her she had never seen a couple so in love. So too, my mother wrote in her journal (something she put together for her family in the early 2000s), 'we had no money, but we were idyllically happy'.

I ask now, what happened to this love? What went wrong? Peggy suggested my father arrived back from the Second World War a changed man. My mother was possibly a changed woman: she had an affair with an American marine while my father was away. I wonder now, perhaps these were just excuses conjured up by a woman with a guilty secret.

When my father returned from the Second World War, he took up an apprenticeship as a bricklayer. Eventually, he went into business for himself and became a successful craftsman. He trained apprentices and was highly thought of as a tradesman – certainly in his younger years. He had taken full advantage of the New Zealand Government's offer to returned servicemen of financial help and training in various work skills.

It was into this world I was born. My mother writes in her journal, of the delight in bringing me into the world. It was, she says, 'a wonderful experience … there was so much joy in caring for this baby'.

She was also concerned about their lack of finances. She recalled the exact amount of money they had to live on and commented, 'Into this world of poverty yet contentment and happiness, arrived Kay'. I have some charming photographs of my parents and myself – in one of them, my father holds me in his arms and smiles down at me as though I am very much his pride and joy. What happened for this idyllic existence to disappear?

In recent years, a psychic told me my destiny was stolen from me. She said someone saw the three of us in our blissful state together and became jealous. As a result, this person cast a spell on us, and our lives were changed for ever. While this story would make a good introduction to a movie, I very much doubt its authenticity. The reality of the situation was, I am sure, much more down to earth.

Just before my third birthday, my little brother was born. With a second baby on the scene did life simply become too difficult for my parents? That is no excuse for what happened around this time. We were living in a dark little flat which joined onto another flat and there would have been nothing joyous about this environment for my parents. It is noticeable that all the family photographs from this period are taken outdoors.

One of the memories my mother was prepared to talk about from this time, is of my walking down a long hallway in a pair of her high-heel shoes making an enormous clatter on the bare floorboards. Although she knew it would have been an unpleasant noise for her next-door neighbour, she did nothing to stop the constant banging. It kept me happy, and this is what she wanted. Perhaps this is the first hint of her tendency to be self-centred. It also tells me my love of shoes started at a very young age. At the time, my parents were preparing to move from this flat to a new house my father was building.

Before we moved, a life-changing incident occurred in that gloomy abode. In a flash, my happy little life was transformed. My father touched me inappropriately. I have no idea what motivated him or indeed how many times he touched me. Although I did not remember this until much later as a fifty-something woman, the image that came to me was very clear. It was after a healing session with a Reiki Master that slowly, over a period of a few months, the picture crystalised: I saw my father leaning over my little body touching my private parts and looking into my eyes and smiling at me. Or was it more of a leer? At the same time, I am looking up at him with dread, and trying to sink into the mattress of my cot. I thought I recalled saying to myself at the time, *you shouldn't be doing this, Daddy*. However, a counsellor told me this was my adult mind encroaching on the remembered image. I was apparently too young to be so aware of his wrongdoings. The picture of the cot is a very distinct image and although I might have been a little old for sleeping in one, my parent's poverty would have ensured I slept in this bed, certainly until we moved house.

I have examined the figures and know he first touched me when I was around three years old. My mother confirmed that during my first years, I was a very happy child but around the age of three I began to cry a lot. What adds to the trauma of this 'touching' is my mother was part of the image. The picture, which is as distinct today as when I first saw it over twenty years ago, has my mother holding a baby – my little brother – in her arms as she stands in the darkened hallway peering round the doorway into the bedroom. She was watching my father touch me. Like the picture of my mother, the image of my father hovering over my body is still with me if I want to go there. And that look is etched on my psyche.

With the move to our new house, I had a new bed. I even had my own bedroom with two built-in beds with book shelves over the top. The cot was gone, no doubt being used by my brother who was now about nine months old and in his own bedroom. My parents, too, had a built-in bed with book shelves over the top and they had special side tables that matched their bed. I note these small details because they will become important to the story that will eventually unfold.

My parents were fortunate enough to buy a piece of land in an area in Auckland which had been opened up and designated for returned servicemen. All the houses were newly built, and the gardens were only recently established. Everything was new.

The neighbours, primarily with young families, had much in common. Comradeship was easily established, especially with the help of the home-made beer they all became involved in making. Their Saturday afternoon drinking, usually in one of their gardens, could turn into more serious partying. Sometimes they met simply to play cards, other times it was loud music and dancing. Always, though, there was a lot of drink involved. Peggy once told me her early years of partying with the neighbours were 'the worst years of my life'.

In her journal, she wrote a note about this part of her life. She began by recalling details of life with my father:

'He worked hard, so very hard, often giving up his weekends to work. He was generous with his time and money and was a good provider ... I know in later years he 'played' hard, and I never knew what he would get up to, but in spite of that, he was a loving husband and father. I only like to remember the good things about him, though at times I often have unpleasant dreams about his drink and driving. They were a nightmare to me latterly, and even last night I had an awful dream about his drink. All dreams about him aren't unpleasant though.'

This was written a decade after my father died. Her composure in detailing both the positive and negative thoughts she held about her husband suggests an even-handedness in her remembering. Or was she trying to change our family history? Was it only my father's excess drinking which worried away at her? A little further on in her journal, she harks back to their early days, and I wonder if she is hinting about my father's depravities. She writes:

'Our worse [sic] years were when a group of us started making home brew. We all neglected our children at that time. It's too painful to think about, let alone write about.'

It was during this period diabolical things happened in our family, but my mother kept the secret tight within herself until the day she died. It was also around this time I heard the recording of *The Snow Goose* – a life-shaping moment for me. Good can happen even when bad things are occurring.

I remember one of those Saturday nights; my father's older sister, our Auntie Joyce, arrived to stay with us. The sun was just beginning to go down, and Joyce found my brother and I by ourselves in the lounge room, quietly reading. Apparently, there was loud music coming from a distance. Joyce settled us into bed and stomped off to the house the loud music was coming from. Annoyed that we children had been left on our own, she stormed into the party only to be told that throughout the night all the children were checked on. It was a regular feature. One of the men would inspect the houses to ensure the children, most of whom were under ten years old, were all right, in their beds, and hopefully asleep. I do not consider there was anything sinister about this checking of the children. Obviously, Auntie Joyce was concerned to think we had been left unattended. Perhaps there was an element of the unknown still, in such a newly opened area. This checking of the children was to become significant for my mother in her later years because it gave her the means to dissemble events from this period.

On another Saturday night, when they were gathered at our home, I was privy to how they could party. It was riotous. I remember them playing musical cushions which even then was a game usually associated with children. How they enjoyed it – running around and bumping into each other once the music stopped.

It was not all fun and games though. At this same party, I happened to catch an undercurrent at play. I saw my mother standing at the kitchen bar with a small crystal-like glass in her hand, and she was crushing it between her fingers. I can still see her holding that gold-tipped whisky glass. In later years Peggy confirmed her crushing of the glass and explained it was in that moment she realised she had had enough of all the drinking and games. I think there was more than games involved. My mother hinted at an affair she had with one of the men although she never gave me any details. Eventually, the parties must have come to an end, although my father's heavy drinking carried on, usually with his work mates.

The effect his drinking had on me is evident when on one occasion I took it into my head to pour all the beer out of the bottles stored under our house. This would bring the drinking to an end, I thought. One of my father's work mates caught me in the act. The drinking continued for the rest of his life. I am sure he was an alcoholic although it was never spoken of. He knew no control – he had never understood boundaries – and was often unable to walk properly after drinking bouts which certainly happened most weekends.

It must be said my father was not all bad. The good things I remember about him include the many times he would gather my brother and me and my cousins around him and tell us his made-up fairy stories, usually about pirates and princesses. I dare not investigate the symbolism in the stories he told, but he could keep us enthralled for what seemed like hours. Then there was his generosity with money. He did not seem to have a mean streak in him. Any cash he received from work he did was simply handed straight over to my mother to control.

Some people held my father in high regard, and I have just been reminded of this. There is a small book of poems on my bookshelf, written by an Auckland academic my father did some work for. Here he is lauded in a special poem she called *The Stonemason*. They obviously worked together building her wall, and she wrote about how they worked together 'in perfect harmony'.

Another factor about my father is he did not care what others thought of him. His work van was a battered old thing, and he would joke about the only way he could stop it was to put his feet through the floorboards. This van was a most unwelcome addition to his golf club parking lot, but it did not bother him.

Further, there are a couple of stories from my early years which show his caring side. When I was eight years old there was one occasion when I wanted to go to church. It was my father who took me – Peggy was not interested. Going to church to 'thank God' is something I have done periodically throughout my life. For instance, when I recovered from breast cancer, as a fifty-year-old, off I went to church.

Another story comes from the time I was twelve or thirteen years old. One morning I sat on my bed and refused to go to school. I do not recall what had caused me to shut down, but I do remember what I was thinking at the time: I could sit for ever like this, dumb, not speaking and never needing to talk again. My young head seemed to be contemplating this as a very comfortable thing to do. With my new-found awareness, I am wondering if there was something more sinister about my shutting down. I have no recollection of what pushed me to find a more secure place inside myself. It was my father who came to my rescue. I remember him kneeling on the floor with a glass of whisky in his hand quietly trying to talk some sense into me and encouraging me to take a sip of the whisky. He obviously thought the whisky would relax and perhaps brighten me up. I tell this story to highlight my father's caring side and because my mother was nowhere around. She probably thought I was having one of my highly strung moments as she called them.

Our father was the parent who nursed our hurts. If either my brother or I fell and bruised ourselves, a bowl with disinfected water was made ready and he would gently try to wipe our pain away. It was always our father who embraced us with his care in this way. I question where my mother was at these times. Her journal provides a possible answer. In it, she relates all the many wonderful adventures she and her siblings experienced with their father, such as pigeon shooting and walking for miles over sandhills looking for Māori stones and curios, and then Peggy says of her mother:

> 'I don't remember much about my mother, or my relationship with her. She probably cooked our meals and clothed us, but there was no relationship with her that I can remember like there was with our father.'

Perhaps she followed in her own mother's footsteps.

My early childhood years are primarily like a wasteland. Memories have deserted me. I do remember, though, that our childhood holidays were always enjoyable. We had cousins who were of a similar age and our two families would go off to the beach camping for a couple of weeks in summer. There was plenty of swimming and lazing around on the beach and we all became very good at building sand castles. Often Christmas was spent in a tent by the beach and always we celebrated it with our cousins, the children of my mother's sister. It was a carefree and fun time.

I do not remember any violence in our house except once, when I saw my father beating my brother, Douglas. He was a little scallywag, of the sort that had no fear of lighting a fire under a neighbour's house. Perhaps it was this incident the beating was about. I remember writing him a note at the time telling him how much I loved him and how sorry I was he had been hurt by our father.

I do not remember any arguments between my parents. If there were any disagreements in our family, they would usually stem from me and a specific gripe I had with my father, not that I can recall anything in much detail. One occasion I do remember, and it is not something I am particularly proud of. We were sitting at the dinner table, and something had so aggravated me that I took a swipe at one of the dinner plates only for it, and all the food, to land on the floor. I was around nine years old and should have known better. My punishment, which I was probably quite happy about, was to be sent to my bedroom. It probably got me away from an unhappy situation.

The loss of my dog, Prince, is quite prominent in my memory. One year my parents went away in the shooting season without us children. This was an annual event during the month of May. We would go north to my mother's family where the men would shoot ducks and peasants. A dog could be useful in bringing the birds back to the shooters and this particular year my parents took Prince with them. Perhaps Prince was not a good gun dog because they left him on a farm. I remember being almost hysterical over my loss. I thought, how could my parents do this to me? I wonder if this dog had given me the feeling of warmth and love I was possibly missing from my home life. With hindsight, I can see how important my dog's unconditional love would have felt to me. That I can recall this incident suggests its significance to me.

Then my nana died. I was ten years old, and our world changed for ever. Peggy turned to the Christian church on the death of her mother. I have wondered if my mother lost the one thing that had kept her on an even keel while she was drinking and partying. Had her mother become a stabilising influence on Peggy? Her early lack of any relationship with my nana had obviously changed through the years. Did the loss of her mother send Peggy into a panic to find some other source of comfort? She wrote in her journal, about how her world fell apart at this time. My mother was not known for being emotionally connected to anyone.

Perhaps over time, and with hindsight, I wonder if something special occurred between this mother and daughter. Had her mother been the one person she could talk to about her chaotic life? Nana had been instrumental in controlling Peggy's life at a particular time in the early relationship between my parents. The affair my mother had with the American marine during the war was terminated by Nana. The marine wrote several letters to my mother when he returned to the United States and Nana intercepted and destroyed them.

Once, during our talks together, and I cannot recall why she opened up to me on this matter, my mother commented she learnt all she knew about sex from her American lover. An indication possibly of more than a casual acquaintance. And certainly, evidence the Don Juan my father thought himself to be, was far from a reality. Without her mother to confide in, did Peggy look elsewhere for guidance?

Peggy heard the words that changed her life at the funeral of her mother. She could not remember the actual words she heard the clergyman repeating but she knew they were the words of Jesus. She told me the words touched her soul. She also remembered walking away by herself after the funeral service wondering, *Is that possible, is that really possible?* I suspect, because of what I now know, the words she heard at the funeral revolved round sin and forgiveness, although I cannot be sure of this. As the idea of redemption is a central pillar of Christianity, I think my deduction is close to being correct. A Christian conversion followed as she looked out the kitchen window of our house. Apparently, she had been praying, stood up, and then experienced what she called an expansion of consciousness.

My mother may have changed her outlook to become a Christian, but her personality stayed the same. There is a quite strong memory I have of her around this time. My nana was a sophisticated woman who was still working when she died. Peggy seemed to have gathered all Nana's beautiful clothes together, and one afternoon I watched as my mother paraded in front of her bedroom mirror, changing from one garment to another. My feeling of being left out was quite intense. I made a comment to her about not having even one dress to wear. It was the feeling of not being noticed I remember, not what she may or may not have done about my lack of dresses. There must be a reason for this memory and perhaps it is because it demonstrates the self-centred attitude that was to dominate my mother as she pursued her spiritual journey.

It would be unfair of me not to mention the beautiful embroidery she occasionally worked into my dresses when I was a little girl. Her workmanship was delicate and quite exquisite.

Her deep immersion into the Christian church brought the whole family into its orbit. She became the secretary to the local vicar and taught in the weekly Sunday school programme. After an extended period of study, she gained the diploma necessary to teach religion in schools. I recall she would sit in the family sunroom surrounded by books as she studied. Like me, she was a born student.

Christian activities became a way of life for the whole family. Even my father was on duty at the entrance to the church on a Sunday morning: he called himself the chief chucker-out. And my brother was an altar boy during church services.

I do not remember much about these times and myself. I think I taught at Sunday school for a period but there is very little around the church activities within our family which seem significant to me. The one plus about being involved in the church, for me, is my parents were able to send me to what was considered a highly desirable school. It was a Christian girls' school, and although we were not of the social standing to normally attend a school of this type, the vicar was prepared to vouch for me. I have been quite scathing of being sent there – the education, then, was more about turning us into 'ladies' than obtaining a decent education. My mother never regretted her decision although I think my education would have been more challenging if I had been in the cut and thrust of the public school system.

Even so, my school years were enjoyable. I was a good student, and sports played a central part at my school. Swimming and diving were important to me and throughout the years I was picked to be in the swimming team, eventually becoming swimming captain in my last year at school. My father encouraged me in these water events. He had been a very good board diver himself and spent many hours training me at the local baths. I do not believe there was anything suspicious around his behaviour with me in my swimming costume. Our past was, by now, history.

Although I was the strong leading type at my girls-only school – always captain of the class and a prefect in my last year – my teenage years were not easy. This is probably normal for most teenagers. My problem was I did not really understand boys, although I had a variety of boyfriends. There was no advice from my parents, and I struggled through these years. Fortunately, my first real boyfriend was a very nice young man. We both had a healthy interest in the surfing world and spent a lot of time at the beach. Perhaps his influence on my life helped me navigate my way through the area of my life – sexual relations – that was so challenging for me.

Later I had difficulty fending boys off. I think I was seen as an easy target, although really, I was not. I simply did not know how to handle their attention or myself. Of course, I had not been taught about boundaries – quite the opposite. The black looks I could so easily conjure up were legendary, but I realise now I had a lot to be black about.

Throughout these difficult teenage years, my mother was ensconced in the Christian church. It was her whole life. I do remember her looking after me, though, when I was sitting important exams; she used to cook special brain food for me.

By the end of my schooling, Peggy was earning money as a secretary at the local police station. My brother had been sent to a private boys' school, so she went out to work to help pay for our schooling. Although my father was the big provider, two children at private schools would have been a drain on the family finances. I was the least of my mother's worries.

Once I left home to study physiotherapy at university, I was an accident waiting to happen. I realise now the confusion around sex with which I had grown up had left me incapable of saying the word no. While this is certainly a consideration for why I became pregnant at this time, what was also significant is the era I was living through. The 1960s was a period of great social change when young people like myself were challenging traditional values. Talking with friends my age today, I realise there were many unwanted pregnancies around this time. It was not that we became raving sex maniacs, it was an age of testing the boundaries and experimenting with the idea of freedom from family restrictions.

Another factor was the lack of any education around the issue of sexual relations. It was only through our parents we learnt about these matters. I remember my mother gave me a little booklet and left it at that. Even though the oral contraceptive pill had become commercially available in the mid-1960s, birth control was not a subject for discussion. An article in the American Readers Digest in 1968 makes clear how people generally thought about 'the pill'. Its impact upon society was not only negative but was described as potentially being more devastating than the nuclear bomb. A combination of these circumstances heralded in what was called the sexual revolution and my friends and I were in the thick of it.

The man I was involved with when I became pregnant was another very nice man who wanted to marry me, but I did not seem able to contemplate such a move. I can remember there was no emotion on my part about making the decision to have an abortion. It was a straightforward question of not wanting to start married life in this way.

With hindsight, I recognise there was much more involved in this decision than I admitted to, or even knew about at the time. Unbeknown to me, I had learnt in my early years how to keep unwanted emotions in check. Disconnect and freeze out all thoughts and feelings and you could take anything that was thrown at you. I became very good at this emotional immobilisation which must have been very useful around this period of my life.

I did not tell my parents about the pregnancy and handled it alone. Not an easy thing to do in the 1960s. The decision to keep my predicament to myself demonstrates the lack of trust I had in my parents, although at the time I had no deep understanding of why this was so. Fortunately, there have never been any regrets around making this life-determining decision and the man, Steve, stayed friends with me for a further decade, until he married. In due course, he was to be instrumental in one of my life-changing decisions.

Eventually, I set out for London and the big tour of Europe. Physiotherapy was not for me. Apart from the fact that I did not pass the required exams, it did not really appeal. Later, when I returned to university, I realised my interest was caught by ideas and analysis rather than the facts of the body. I did not take the boat over to England like most of my girlfriends. I had a business course to finish and exams to pass. Once done, I flew to Europe via Japan and Russia at a time when flying was only just beginning to become popular generally.

What made me decide to go to Europe through what was then the

Soviet Union I cannot explain. It was a bold step for the period and especially for one so young – and travelling alone. Perhaps this, the world's first Marxist-Communist state, appealed to the latent historian in me. What could I learn about life controlled by such a government?

One outstanding memory from this time is watching the Bolshoi Ballet perform *Swan Lake* in their famous Moscow theatre. There were many ordinary, down-to-earth-looking Russians attending, and how they loved their ballet. So many flowers were thrown onto the stage at the end of the performance. It is a lovely memory.

Another moment in Moscow, although memorable, was not so pleasant. I was charged with stealing the towel from my hotel room. The towel episode provides a sense of this repressive regime. The towel I was provided with was a threadbare piece of cloth and I decided to use the towel I had brought from home. My hotel had a female attendant positioned at the end of the corridor on each floor. She must have entered the room I had exited on my way to the hotel lobby to catch a flight out of the country. The attendant saw there was no towel in my room and came running after me waving her hands and shouting at me. After much agitation, the situation was sorted out. There was no towel in my room to be taken. The cleaning staff had noticed I had not used their tatty towel and had not bothered to leave one in my room.

I was very fortunate to meet an Australian businessman in Moscow who took me under his wing. He had access to the better resources on offer to tourists of the Soviet Union at the time. 'Intourist' was a type of travel agency that provided tourist packages to foreigners visiting Moscow. While I was on a less expensive and low-status package, the businessman was on the top grade. He had a car and driver and access to places I probably was unable to go to by myself. I think it was my friend who managed to obtain the tickets for us to see the Bolshoi Ballet. I remember having a good meal at his top-tier hotel as opposed to my much lower-grade hotel where black bread was the stable fare for breakfast. He certainly made my stay in Moscow more enjoyable, and he probably welcomed having my company.

To reach the three girlfriends who were waiting for me in Dusseldorf in West Germany, I had to fly from Moscow to East Berlin, take a coach through the then Berlin Wall and from West Berlin fly to Dusseldorf. The Berlin Wall was a guarded concrete barrier that encircled West Berlin from 1961 to 1989. I remember being in the coach with other travellers traversing Berlin; the feeling of oppression and being closed in was there for any to feel during that drive. I contemplate these escapades in the Soviet Union now and think this was so adventurous. My only excuse for such daring is that I was young and did not know any better.

In Dusseldorf, and now in the safety of numbers with my girlfriends, we bought a Volkswagen car and camping equipment and set off for three months travelling through Europe. It was 1968, and all sorts of happenings were occurring in Europe. I remember two of us trying to sell our blood in Spain, which was relatively easy to do and quite common at the time. Our money must have been running short, but it turned out we were not heavy enough. Well, that is what we were told.

Our last call was Paris. Here we had just missed the demonstrations and occupations of universities and factories – now called 'May 1968'. I do not remember any civil unrest, just a pure enjoyment to be in this 'City of Light'. To this day I am still delighted when visiting Paris.

Once in London, one of my girlfriends and I rented a flat in a street off the King's Road in Chelsea. We were at the very centre of what was called the 'Swinging Sixties'. This was a period when everything changed. The bleakness of post-war London changed into a place of psychedelic colour. Mary Quant, the creator of the mini skirt, had set up her boutique

BAZAR on the King's Road. The songs of the Beatles were everywhere, and feminism was beginning to gain recognition. We did not realise we were living in such an exuberant and vibrant period. It is only on looking back that I recognise how lucky we were to be experiencing these exciting changes.

Unlike my girlfriends, there was a recognition on my part that there was more than the usual overseas holiday involved in my journey. I must have been talking about spending a few years in London because one of my male friends confided in me he thought I was leaving New Zealand because of my father. I had no idea what he was talking about, and I still wonder what he was getting at. What did he know about my father? Perhaps it was his extensive drinking this friend thought worried me. I ponder on this now and think my father's blatant sexual misbehaviour must have been known by many in Auckland at the time.

In London, I met my first husband, Bill. He was good-looking and seemed to be a sophisticated man of the world. Just what I needed for the beginning of my new life away from New Zealand. He worked as a salesman for IBM, which at the time was one of the biggest office machine companies in the world. Computers and all the accompanying activities surrounding them were in their early days. IBM was in the thick of it. This was the era when the computer had a special air-conditioned room built to house it, and the people who looked after these big machines were deemed gods.

Once married, Bill and I decided to go into business together. With a partner, we bought some second-hand IBM Flexi-writers and offered a service to those companies using the computers. We began punching out (typing) edge punched cards for the new type of office machines, and the paper tape which contained the information needed to operate the big computers. One particularly difficult job we would often be given was punching into paper tape the various programming languages which were often simply big chunks of code. To the ordinary eye, there was no sense to what we were having to type, but these were the instructions to the computer and needed to be absolutely correct. We must have been good at this challenging job because the work kept coming.

It was an exciting time although a lot of hard work. We had married women typists working these machines all over the place – in our work place and at their homes. A telling anecdote from this period is that if we were talking socially and happened to mention we worked in the world of computers, the conversation would end abruptly. It is difficult to imagine, but this was a world very few people were familiar with or even understood at the time. There were still a few years to go before personal computers were to come onto the market and into everyday life.

Bill and I worked well together and with a lot of hard work, often working long hours to meet the deadlines our clients asked for, the business became a success. During this time, I remember the many meals we shared in the late hours of the night, usually at one of the local steakhouses. Chinese restaurants were the only other alternative for casual eating in suburban London during the 1970s. The odd meal we managed to have at home was almost cause for celebration. I also recall being told by my doctor to have that very English of drinks, a sherry, to help me relax of an evening.

Our personal life, though, was based on the acknowledgement that neither one of us wanted children. At this stage, I did not know enough about why it was I did not want children, although I had grown up thinking they were not for me. I do not know why not having children was so important to Bill. Like a lot in my life, this was a personal issue and therefore not discussed. Our marriage was made from the mutual desire not to have children and it worked for both of us for a time. We travelled extensively in Europe and were able to visit New Zealand every other year.

During the twelve-year period I was living in London, my mother was venturing into all things religious in Auckland. Before I left for London she had already walked away from the Christian church. She had read the words from the Bible, which were apparently said by Jesus, 'the kingdom of God is within you'. She promptly set out to find this 'kingdom of God'. The priests of the church were unable to help her in this search. They told her what she was looking for could be found in church and she sensibly did not accept their counsel. So began her journey which I would later write about in such detail.

The first group she joined were students of the Russian philosopher, Gurdjieff. After four years, something of a personal nature happened within this group and my mother left. She refused to talk about this time, but my guess is she may have overworked her charm.

Co-Freemasonry and the Theosophical Society came next. I have a recollection of Peggy dressed in all her white attire as she prepared to go off to one of her masonry meetings. It was as though she was about to attend a ball.

Always during these years, there was the constant learning of ritual which she was so very good at. Whenever I arrived from London there would always be something she was learning by heart. Through the years she took part in all sorts of new-age activities. For instance, she was a regular attendee of Vipassana retreats. The 'Course of Miracles' was no stranger to her, nor was Eckhard Tolle. It had all started with the Christian church where she had engaged with not only the High Anglican Church but also the Jehovah's Witness Church.

The most important influence on her religious life, after the Christian church, was Zen Buddhism. For twenty years she was deeply and wholly involved in it. She refused to call it a religion, instead insisting it was a way of life. She went on retreat once a year, sometimes more, and often was away at an overseas monastery. I experienced one of their local meetings in Auckland, where those attending were all dressed like monks and chanted together as they moved round in a circle. I walked with them on this occasion, and I must confess to not being able to follow their routine as I ended up bumping into them as I walked the wrong way round. The rituals of Buddhism were not for me.

Always though, when I arrived from London my mother tried her best to interest me in whatever was her latest religious preoccupation. I wonder now, just what was holding my mother in organisations like these. Was there something about formalities like Buddhist chanting and the practice of Co-Freemasons that held some distinctive offering for my mother? Did this rigid learning and deep involvement keep her from going into a past she would rather forget? For over fifty years she had tried it all. What was all this journeying about? I had a long way to go before I would understand.

Back in London, our world was changing. The computer industry was growing up, and our business required further investment to keep going. I had had enough of working long hours and was prepared to go out and get a job. Bill was thirteen years older than me and did not fancy the idea of working for anyone again. Gradually my world became grey. It was not only our relationship which changed but the English people and, of course, the weather began to look very grey to me. I hankered after the blue skies of the southern hemisphere. I tried an experiment one Saturday morning to see if it was all in my head. Was this greyness simply my imagination? I dressed up in clothes I thought would bring attention to myself and went shopping. My aim was to see if anyone would notice me in my bright colours. My top was emerald green and my pants a navy blue – believe me, this was bright for England at the beginning of winter. There was no grey or black anywhere on me. And no one took any notice of my brightness. It was not just in my head.

It was more than blue skies I yearned for. My friend, Steve, had been in and out of my life on a casual basis during my marriage to Bill. The one and only English football (soccer) match I have watched live, was with Steve. It is interesting for me to recall this experience – many, many years have passed since I have thought of this event. We had such a good time. The match was being played at the Stamford Bridge Stadium in Fulham. There were police on horses and Chelsea football fans everywhere – the atmosphere was electric.

My good times with Steve changed when we became lovers again. With this change, I knew my marriage to Bill was over. I even began to think it was possible for me to have children with Steve, although he knew nothing of my thoughts on the matter.

It was very difficult to tell Bill of my decision to return to New Zealand. He was just such a good man. Perhaps he could be a little boring at times, but he was reliable and trustworthy.

There was nothing uninteresting or boring about the trips across the English Channel he occasionally took us on in our twenty-two-foot yacht. If we were away for only a few days, Cherbourg on the Normandy coast of France was our port of call. There we would eat some lovely food and then sail back home to England. For longer periods we would go further down the French coast to Le Havre, or across to the Channel Islands. Now, when I think about us doing these extensive trips in such a small boat, it seems so adventurous, but we thought nothing of it. He loved his sailing, and I was his very willing companion.

Bill knew of my relationship with Steve and even suggested he would accept other men in my life if I would be prepared to stay with him. I think he was saying to me 'as long as you're happy I will be happy'. He was the one significant man in my life who was least like my father. I have heard that women either marry men like their fathers or the opposite. Bill was the exact opposite and we remained friends until he died many years later.

On my arrival back in New Zealand, things did not work out between Steve and myself. I did not know he already had someone he was going to marry. Now I recognise this was the first of those times when the man in my life had another woman. I do not recall any emotional dramas at the time. I was young, I think I simply got on with life. I am sure my ability to emotionally disconnect would have helped me once again.

In Auckland, it was easy for me to pick up a job within the expanding computer industry. A lack of satisfaction for me within the computer world meant I stayed one year only, but also my move from London was too much of a change. There was something of a small-town atmosphere in Auckland at the time. Further, my brother was a popular rugby player, and I became known as his sister. I look at this now and wonder if once again there was more to this feeling than I knew about. I remember when I first arrived in London there was a wonderful sense of freedom around the awareness that I was unknown and knew no one. Was my background – the desire to fly away high and free – imposing itself unknowingly upon my decisions? Sydney seemed big enough.

I flew back to see Bill in England before flying off to Sydney, where a girlfriend helped me settle in. Here I bought myself a house from the split-up of the finances Bill and I had shared. Once again, I was offered what I seem to remember was a high-powered job with the newly formed Apple Computers. I turned the offer down and began to sell real estate. This job did not last long either as I began to see myself becoming like the other real estate agents – anything for a deal. By then I had already met the man who was to become my second husband.

Jamie was another older man. I recognised during these years my penchant for older men and always put it down to finding them more interesting. Younger men had not lived as much and were not so stimulating to me – I thought. Now I can see the desire for a caring father figure is obvious in the decisions I made about who I married. And these two men were the only ones I have truly trusted. Jamie was fifteen years older, a bon vivant and great fun. Like my father, he had an allure about him. In appearance he looked rather like a modern-day Edward VII – he had a beard, was not tall (he would not like to be called short) and had a hint of dandyism in the way he dressed. The drama missing from my life with Bill was here in spades with Jamie. On one of our visits to Auckland, Peggy commented on the constant stream of laughter coming from her upstairs living area when we were there.

Our life together was very comfortable. Jamie already had children from his previous marriage, and although we discussed the possibility of having children together it was not a priority for him, and of course, I was happy to go along with the decision not to have them.

He worked and travelled within the decorative arts, and I would usually accompany him on his overseas trips. On one trip to Paris, I recall we were walking down the street arm in arm – I was wearing my red French beret which I still wear to this day and Jamie was looking his usual debonaire self. An elderly Frenchman walked past us murmuring "*Très charmant.*" We obviously looked the part. But then we generally enjoyed ourselves wherever we were.

Once I began my university studies, Jamie was very supportive, and when I received my PhD, he was obviously very proud of my achievement. Intellectually we were a good match although around words he was almost at genius level. I was not. One quite endearing routine we developed while I was writing my PhD was my using him as a thesaurus. This was the period before laptops with their built-in thesaurus facility. I worked upstairs in the study and if he was home, he would be downstairs, usually on the terrace. We had an open-plan house, and I would call down asking for another word to replace the one I already had. Always, he would come back with a different word.

Early on in my study, he demonstrated great respect for what I was doing. I was given extra time to complete my first history essay because we were going to Europe during the university holidays. The essay accompanied us on our holiday and once it was finished, I gave it to Jamie to read – he would always check my spelling and grammar. His response was, 'but you haven't answered the question'. He was right of course. For the rest of our holiday, I was rejigging my essay. There were no complaints from Jamie, simply an acceptance of my preoccupation with my university work. A note I made in my journal almost a decade after he died points to the fundamentals of our relationship. I wrote:

> 'It is my darling's birthday. Oh, what he gave me. Not only financial security but intellectual security as well – his acceptance and enjoyment of my studying was indeed a great gift. He was strong in that part of his life but not so strong emotionally. Jealousy was part of his make-up with me. Perhaps understandable in an older man. Am sure we were meant to meet up.'

Fortunately, there was never any incident involving jealousy – other men were not my interest.

Yet, our life together was not all sunny. There were arguments that seemed to arrive out of nowhere. Suddenly there was a squabble – no, it was more than simply a squabble – without my knowing why. I am trying to recall what these disagreements were about but nothing specific comes to mind. I do not think they were of any great importance except perhaps as a reminder to me to be careful.

One birthday I do remember there was an unpleasant conflict. He did not like the trousers I had picked as a present from him. I kept them for a day and then took them back to the shop. I now recognise this as a controlling mechanism on his part, but at the time any appreciation of what was involved in these encounters was beyond me. The technique of disconnecting I was so skilled at came in very useful at these times, although towards the end of our life together these blots on our existence began to diminish our relationship.

There were times I wondered what the connection was between Jamie and my father. I knew there was a similarity but could not work it out. They both drank quite a bit. I knew in his previous marriage he had been what I called a serial adulterer. I also understood he would not have kept this habit only for his first marriage. I was saved from the pain of facing adultery in our relationship because he became impotent. I suspect he might have tried to make sexual overtures to other women, but I do not have any details to hand. Of course, this sort of predatory behaviour was exactly what my father was deeply entangled in for most of his life, and this was the similarity between my father and my husband I had struggled to identify. However, while Jamie was alive, I did not venture into my deep past and the little that had been revealed was forgotten. Understanding has arrived only as I have worked through the issues of my life in the last year.

A Revelation

It was my mother who originally led me to uncover the secrets within our family. I developed breast cancer in 1992 and Peggy flew to Sydney to spend time with me and, unusually for her, to mother me. She cooked special food for me and prepared a beetroot juice which was meant to be beneficial for fighting cancer. To this day I struggle to swallow this drink.

Peggy appeared quite shocked to think I could have cancer. Her mother had died of the disease at a relatively young age, and she saw my situation as similar. It was not. The cancer in my breast was caught in its early stages, unlike Nana who had cancer throughout her body. No doubt adding to my mother's concern for me was the fact that her sister and my cousin (one of my early childhood playmates) had developed cancer. Was there a family connection with cancer? Much later it was discovered there was a genetic component to the cancer that ran through my aunt's family line. Peggy had good reason to be concerned.

Fortunately, I knew a very good acupuncturist practising in Sydney at the time. I was into alternative medicine and asked him to help me. The acupuncturist made me read Bernie Siegel's book, *Love, Medicine, and Miracles*, published in 1986 before he would treat me. Siegel argued breast cancer was caused by emotional turmoil, and remission of cancer was possible if a patient gave up emotional repression. Emotional control was the story of my life although at the time I had very little understanding of what was personally involved. Recent studies have used different words but express a similar sentiment. The inability to communicate emotion, particularly feelings associated with anger, has been identified as a risk factor for cancer. It is obvious to me now that my body was easy prey for breast cancer to develop.

My mother was so badly shaken by my diagnosis she let her guard down about our family. It was only a little breakdown, but it was enough to start a tsunami – for me anyway. She voiced her concern about the cancer possibly having something to do with my relationship with my father. I can remember very clearly where we were sitting (looking out over Sydney Harbour from my bedroom terrace) and the chairs we were sitting on at the time she said this to me.

How I took this comment is another matter. I do not remember any big discussion about what she really meant. There was simply no questioning on my part. I recollect thinking her comment was a little strange, although, throughout my life at home I had trouble getting on with my father so I thought this must be what she was talking about. The detail of how I did not get on with my father is difficult to explain. He was always very supportive of me, particularly in sporting activities. Perhaps it is best explained as a tension that was always in my being when I was around him.

Peggy's association of my breast cancer with our family history suggests she was interested in the mind-body connection, which advocates that physical health and emotional health are intimately intertwined. It would have been in the early stage of its development in New Zealand during the 1980s, but then she was always into issues of self-improvement. Books about good nutrition and self-development, such as Dale Carnegie's famous book *How to Win Friends and Influence People*, were on our book shelf. She was obviously influenced by this different way of thinking about the development of disease. That she opened up at this time about the relationship between me and my father – even in such a minor way – suggests how seriously she perceived the mind-body connection. It also indicates how concerned she was for me. She was never to unlock her thoughts on our family secrets again.

Ever the student of new ideas and new ways of being, Peggy began to be involved in the ancient Buddhist practice of Reiki. Briefly, this is a technique said to promote healing and which is based on the life force energy that flows within us. When I visited her in Auckland a few months after her stay in Sydney, she told me of someone who used Reiki to uncover sexual abuse, and she had made an appointment for me to see this woman. At the time I did not see any connection between Peggy's inference about my cancer being linked to our father-daughter relationship and this meeting she had arranged for me. And again, I did not question my mother. It is hard to believe I did not interrogate her at this time. Why did I go so freely to someone considered to be an expert in sexual abuse without any questions? I do not know the answer to this, except that all my reading has led me to now understand how my body remembered the trauma of my early years. I did not need to question my mother because I already knew – unconsciously. Yet at the time, I had no idea of what was coming.

The first session with the Reiki lady was a very peaceful experience of deep meditation. Her room was the essence of tranquillity. I lay on a massage table fully clothed while she stood behind me. A deep feeling of relaxation came over my whole body. My eyes were closed but I understand the process involves the placing of hands lightly on or over particular areas of the body. Research tells me Reiki can help to ease emotional and psychological traumas brought on by difficult life events. Obviously, this is why my mother made the appointment for me.

It was the next session, two days later, which suggested I had been sexually abused. The same procedure occurred although this time the slow realisation of my father's involvement in sexual abuse came to me. It is not easy to explain exactly what happened. Reiki is about energetic elements with the practitioner being the conduit of the energy. I can recall the impressions I received and the image that seemed to form out of nothing. At first, I thought the image slowly coming towards me was my husband. My senses were saying *oh no, oh no,* to the idea this could possibly be Jamie, which leads me to believe I understood in some way that this was about sexual abuse. Slowly the image came closer and closer until it became unmistakeable; my father was standing before me. I acknowledged his appearance with a glum acceptance.

A friend who is familiar with Reiki has explained to me what happened on this fateful day. The deep relaxed state I could so easily achieve with meditation brought with it an acute awareness. Using the plain words of my friend, this state of neither being awake nor asleep enabled the unconscious to rise to the surface. Then the conscious mind was able to access the information hidden in the unconscious. Or to use Jung's words, the process allowed the unconscious to become conscious. This meant the sexual abuse hiding for so long within me, was able to be acknowledged.

With my recognition of the abuse, the Reiki lady then helped me release the trauma of what had been revealed. I took great delight, in my mind, in swirling my abusive father down a plug hole where he disappeared out of sight.

A third session helped me regain the relaxed attitude of mind which accompanied the first session. I was told because of the deep meditation I had practised during my recovery from cancer, the Reiki process had worked very quickly and efficiently. Between the second and third sessions, there was further confirmation about my father from another source.

Previously I had organised to have dinner with one of my cousins, Penny, and coincidentally, or was it, this happened to be on the day the sexual abuse was revealed. Penny was a little older than me and knew my father well as she came from his side of the family. He would often call at her house on a Sunday morning to have a drink. I remember the restaurant we arranged to meet at was Italian, but there is very little else I can recall about our dinner. My head was swirling, and I asked for a glass of wine as soon as I arrived. I knew this was going to be a very difficult conversation.

My initial glum acknowledgement of the sexual abuse was by now transformed into a deep distress. Still, I was determined to find out whatever I could. I can be quite direct at times and true to form I asked Penny, almost as she was sitting down at the table, if she knew anything about sexual abuse surrounding me and my father. The writing of my PhD was proving difficult at the time – I seemed to be blocked – so I suggested to her I needed clarification about his behaviour because the continued writing of my PhD depended upon it. Whether this made it any easier for her or not, I do not know.

Even if Penny had said nothing to me, I could see she knew something because her face immediately gave her away. She went pale before my eyes. She was also very reluctant to talk to me about what she knew, although the few words she did say were, in hindsight, significant. What I did not pick up at the time, but realised much later, was that Penny knew something I was completely oblivious to. My anguish was obvious; she tried calming me and then asked me if my brother was all right. My response was, "What has this got to do with Douglas?" Too caught up in my own drama I did not comprehend that she had added my brother to the abuse. All I knew and accepted, at this stage, was my father had sexually abused me. Nothing else.

I did gather from Penny, that whatever it was she knew about, the situation was treated very light-heartedly. They were probably drinking after all. I never did find out exactly what my father said to her or what she understood to have been involved.

I cannot imagine how we continued with our conversation over dinner. We never returned to the subject, not only because it was obviously too painful for her, but there was also a reluctance on my part to go there. It gradually dawned on me that before our dinner together that night she had not associated sexual abuse with what my father had told her. Hence her absolute dismay on realising she had possibly misinterpreted the situation. She has since died.

My mother's reaction to the illuminating Reiki session was very revealing. I remember she was standing in her kitchen preparing food when I arrived back at the house before I went out to dinner with Penny. Immediately, I told her what had been exposed and all she could do was cry out, "No, no," accompanied by profuse weeping. It was her reaction to my revelation of swirling my father down the plug hole which was most telling. She was most upset I could even think of doing such a thing to him. Her lack of any concern for me at the time did not touch me, it is only as I write out these details that I feel slightly angry and wonder what was going on for her. I think she had already made plans in her head about what she would say whenever the sexual abuse was revealed. After all, she had sent me to an expert on sexual abuse. She did not try to denounce the idea of my having been sexually abused, she simply tried to pass it off as something that could have happened during their partying days. It was the evening check on the children sleeping in their beds she held responsible. She said one of these men could have done something to me.

Later I began to realise that Peggy had adopted a particular man (she dropped his name occasionally) as the scapegoat for the time when inevitably the abuse was revealed. Had she forgotten her worry about the cancer in my body being possibly a connection to the relationship I had with my father? She would not, or could not, acknowledge the possibility of my father's involvement, and continued to quietly deny anything had happened within our family for the rest of her life. The subject did not come up very often because there was very little of a personal nature which passed between Peggy and me.

The revelation of sexual abuse sent me into a spin. More than that, I was shattered, and the conversation with my cousin had not helped.

Once back at the house after dinner the inner turmoil hit me. Coincidentally, I had just finished reading a book in which I thought I had read the author had been sexually abused. Well, I went into a frenzy to try and find the passage where I thought she had revealed how she coped with the revelation. This book could help me, I thought. Page after page was turned in a crazy sort of hysteria: it went on for hours. Over and over through the pages I hunted for a paragraph which quite possibly was not there. I returned to the book days later in a much calmer state and again did not find it. Perhaps the paragraph had been a creation of my imagination and something that helped me vent my feelings. Once I had stopped turning pages there was no way I was going to sleep, so I spent the night walking from one end of the bedroom to the other. It was a small room and I seemed to be physically going round in circles just like the thoughts in my head. Inside my mind, there was a revolving panic, with questions of how, what, where, going round and round. If only my mother had been able to talk with me. This was her chance, but it was not to be.

The following day I had arranged to meet a girlfriend for lunch. I remember feeling extremely flat, my head was still spinning, and I was quite detached from our conversation. I have no idea what we talked about, where we ate or what she thought of my distracted demeanour. I spent the evening with my mother, and nothing was said. I find this difficult to believe now. It was almost as though we had become mute. The one thing at the centre of both our minds at the time had left us speechless. I wonder now why I was not more proactive. I was a thinking woman, part way through researching for and writing a PhD. Why was I seemingly so remote from what had been revealed? I understand now that this was part of the coping mechanism that got me through these traumatic days.

My mother's silence on the matter was followed by that of my husband. The night I arrived back from Auckland we dined out at our favourite Chinese restaurant. Halfway through the meal, I told Jamie what had happened and how I thought my father had sexually abused me. Was he shocked? No – and this was probably because he was very definite about the fact this could not have happened to me. He did acknowledge my father's overwhelming tendency to be a 'womaniser', as he called it, but not in relation to me. He had spent afternoons drinking with my father and knew how he acted when he was around women. He told me, "I can imagine him putting it anywhere but never, never near you." To be fair to Jamie, at this stage, all I knew was that there had been some sort of sexual abuse. I had no details to convince him and could only tell him of the reaction of my cousin Penny, and the involvement of my mother. He was not persuaded, and the subject was never mentioned again. Those who knew in my family – mother, cousin, and husband – remained silent all their lives. But then, I never talked about it either.

It was a few months after the Reiki session when more detailed information arrived. An image began to appear before me –it was unheralded and uncalled for. This was the image of my father bending over my cot, touching me while my mother stood by watching. It developed slowly but surely. And it was very clear. I now know this was the unconscious doing its work. I had accepted the fact of the sexual abuse and now my unconscious was able to bring this ill-fated picture into my conscious mind. I did not panic over this image as I had over the realisation of being sexually abused. Perhaps because it arrived bit by bit, I was able to endure this forlorn picture. I do not remember any agitation at the time – just a gradual acceptance. The image was not there in those first months of revelation. What was with me from the very beginning was the knowledge of my mother's tendency to cover up unpleasant realities. She was into more than covering up, though.

By chance a few years ago I found a letter she had sent me soon after I had visited her in Auckland. I cannot imagine why I kept this letter at the time, but here it was, simply appearing. In the letter she wrote:

> 'You gave me the impression over the phone that the blockage [regarding my PhD] was something to do with your father – what came up in Reiki … thinking about their traumas doesn't help these people who talk and talk about them and keep going to counselling. They need to just take a good look at it and see it disappear. Thinking about anything perpetuates whatever it is – it's not on, really Kay.'

This is the same woman, who on several occasions when I visited Auckland from London, sent me off to a psychic. I realise now – she was sending me off on a possible trip of discovery. It is interesting for me to wonder what my mother thought she was doing sending me to psychics and the Reiki lady. She was living very dangerously. Did she not worry about what could be revealed, or was she simply attempting to purge her guilt? Her inability to accept the revelation from my Reiki experience tells us something – probably that she was in denial – still, I am bewildered by what my mother thought she was doing making these appointments.

Peggy never knew of the image that revealed itself to me. I did not once consider telling her and I wonder why not? She was, of course, part of the image. Was I covering for her? Or was it simply a case of my not being able to confront her? I think about this now and realise the time was not right for me. There was still more to be revealed and a much deeper place for me to have to revisit.

These events were remembered when I was around fifty years old. Then they were pushed into the recesses of my mind for another twenty years. Stored and forgotten. How could this happen? Of course, I was an expert at emotional detachment. This capability, if I dare call it that, certainly enabled me to carry on with my life virtually untainted by what had been revealed.

For the next ten years, Jamie and I lived out our lives happily enough. We sold the lovely house we had built on the edge of Sydney Harbour (we had had enough of the city) and moved to the rainforest area of Tamborine Mountain in Queensland. This was a regional area behind the Gold Coast which I fell in love with while visiting a girlfriend. When I brought Jamie up to this beautiful environment there happened to be an Italian-style house on the market which appealed to his aesthetic leanings. Within months we had moved in.

We both became deeply involved in our different interests. Jamie played bridge a couple of times a week and continued with his extensive reading. I think he knew of every new book that came onto the market. I began to garden in a big way. I created many areas of garden around our new house and even opened the garden to the public, sometimes twice a year, through the local garden club and Australia's Open Garden scheme.

During my first years of gardening a Queensland-based garden club was established with some very experienced gardeners at the helm. There was so much to learn from these knowledgeable women and men.

I also began to write an article for their monthly newsletter, based on the idea that a garden could reveal so much about a person. It was fascinating to see how the gentle and often more spiritual gardeners would concentrate on the paler colours such as pink and blue for their plantings, while someone like myself, a little more fire-like in nature, would be quite happy with red flowers dotted through the garden. Then there were the structured and more contained gardens which hinted at a gardening personality who tended to be organised, rather than the unruliness of plantings everywhere. These beautiful but often chaotic gardens suggested spontaneity and a sense of freedom in an individual. I think there were some ladies who quietly avoided me when I went looking for my next subject to write about. For me, it was my first foray into putting together words after my academic writing and I found it very stimulating.

A few years into our time on Tamborine Mountain Jamie's health deteriorated, and we considered moving to Brisbane to be closer to the medical services he required. At the thought of leaving my garden, I began a journal about the joys of creating a garden and put myself under the same radar of gardening and personality, as I had done with the garden group. It is interesting for me to read this journal now. What I learnt: life and gardening seemed so intertwined. For instance, there is a comment about the colour yellow in my garden. Previously, in Sydney, I had avoided any yellow flowers either for the house inside or for plantings outside. I wrote in my journal:

'I always thought the yellow thing was about the house (it was stone painted yellowy-orange) or even the climate here in Queensland.

But if it was the climate there would be many bright-yellow gardens here – there are not. Therefore, it must have been something about me, my personality. Yellow seems to have a happy feel about it.'

And yes, I was so happy in this garden. Another comment:

'Is interesting to contemplate the mixture of plants. Each big-look plant is lovely by itself but put together they don't mix. Could be a group of people actually – some people do not mix well. In this case of the plants, they are too different. Like humans – too different and they won't mix.'

Another observation was almost like a forewarning of what was to come. I was writing of the many hedges around my garden and their use for achieving privacy:

'I don't know why I want privacy so much. Some people are quite happy to be open to everyone in their house and garden. Someone else will have to work this out for me.'

Now, I understand – my history demanded privacy. We did not sell our house at the time and my garden continued to grow and develop.

What also happened for me in this lovely garden is that I became reacquainted with my love of birds. The story of the snow goose I had heard as a young girl was still deep within me. My garden introduced me to the beautiful bowerbirds and the unique courtship they perform. The handsome-looking blue-black males build a stick structure and decorate it with mainly blue objects such as bottle tops, pieces of straw or laundry pegs. The odd yellow article could also appear amongst the blue. This colourful array of objects is used to entice the lady bowerbirds into the bower. We usually had one big 'proper' bower and then there was another part of the garden used by the young males to practise their bower-building skills. I was quite disturbed to find that occasionally a bower had been destroyed. I thought my dog was giving way to fits of jealousy: that this was his, and only his, garden. It was a relief to find it was usual practice for these young male birds to destroy their structure and then start to build it all over again. I used to sneak up on these bowers but rarely caught the 'builders' at work.

What I did see a lot of was the olive-brown females flying from all angles into and out of our rose garden at dusk. They would swoop over the trees, into the garden and back up to the trees on the other side of the garden, sometimes at least six of them were flying together. The antics of the bowerbirds kept me enthralled right up to when I left this house only a few years ago.

Recently, I have wondered why in the quiet moments of gardening nothing of my past came up to disturb me. Gardening can be a time of deep contemplation when insights can appear out of nowhere. Perhaps I was too busy. But really, once again, I do not think the time was right. Certainly, the last five years of my life with Jamie were very demanding. He had numerous health problems, which often required immediate attention. Frequently we had to make a dash to Brisbane to find treatment. He died in hospital from heart and kidney complications in 2008. In a strange coincidence, he died on my birthday. My ability to detach emotionally helped me to cope with his death, although I remember being quite distraught in the moment of his dying. All I seemed able to do was run from the hospital. It took me two years before I began to really feel my loss, although I have been told I looked ten years older during this period.

It was on the death of Jamie that I had my first encounter with what has become my troublesome heart. I saw a cardiologist for the first time. The emotional detachment I was so skilled at was unable to fool my body. It was only because I started to cry over something silly – a bank document I think it was – I realised I needed emotional help. A grief counsellor helped me through my heartache.

I remember talking with a fellow gardening friend who had also lost her husband and we agreed that there was only one positive to life without our husbands. We could now buy any plant we wanted. Strangely enough, soon after Jamie's death, I lost interest in adding plants to our garden. Perhaps one phase of my life was over, and the next about to begin.

In the past the idea that trauma can be forgotten and then resurface years later was called junk science. This notion has now been debunked. The little research I have carried out on memory suggests that total memory loss is most common in childhood sexual abuse cases. Further, forgetting was more prevalent the younger the abused was and if there was no support from the mother. This helps explain my first fifty years of memory loss. The twenty years after is not so easily understood. Yet, if I go back to that fifty-year-old I realise I dismissed the image of a father touching his little daughter. I could not make sense of it and with no one to talk to, the image became unconsciously internalised again. Only many years later as I began to talk with my mother about her spiritual journey did I begin to untie some of the knots curled up inside me.

Talks With My Mother

In the last decade of her life, my mother left New Zealand and came to Australia to live near me and Jamie. She sold her house in Auckland and bought one in Tamborine Mountain, only a few kilometres away from us. This was a very big thing for her to do as she was very much a New Zealander. She loved her rugby and the New Zealand All Blacks. She said of her eighty-fifth birthday, it would not have been so enjoyable if the All Blacks had lost the game they played on that night. Yet, Peggy had the fortitude to leave all this behind and start a new life in Australia. At the age of eighty-four, she wrote in her journal: 'Wonderful to be here with you Kay – to be with you has made the move to Australia worthwhile.' Although it was a difficult decade in many ways, it was also a good decade for both of us. The best way to describe our relationship at this time is, we became firm friends.

The strength of character which enabled her to change countries at such an age seemed to disappear when her little dog, Charlie, died. He had come with her from New Zealand, and they had spent some wonderful years together. He went everywhere with her in the car and every day they would walk to the local café. When he died her grief was deep and heartfelt. She would cry; more than cry – I was told she could be heard wailing as she walked between her house and the café she visited. Her grief almost overwhelmed her, as did the walks she tried to take to reach the Anglican Church, a good two kilometres away from her house. She also apparently made a nuisance of herself on the telephone with the clergyman. Finally, she found a church near her house, which she could walk to easily, and for the next three years, she attended regularly each Sunday. Slowly the angst about her dog abated and she became firmly entrenched within this local church.

When Peggy arrived in Australia, she was still a practising Zen Buddhist, so her return to the Christian church was a conundrum for me. I was unable to understand why and how she could make such a big shift in her spiritual outlook. However, I must declare my own interest in this matter. The philosophy behind Zen Buddhism seemed more akin to how I saw the world, rather than the Christian church and its religious dictates. Indeed, I was proud of my mother's involvement in Zen Buddhism. Her turn towards Christianity set me on a mission to comprehend her change. Well, this is what I thought I was doing.

So began three years of my literally interviewing her. Almost every word she uttered in response to my questions was written down. We met for coffee, and sometimes lunch, a couple of times a week. Jamie had died so I had as much time as was needed to spend with her. Now and again I was missing a notepad and out would come any piece of paper to write down her latest offerings to me. One of her little gems was written on the back of a real estate agent's card: 'Heaven is a state of being. I have been there – in the silence. You don't go to it – it happens.'

Sometimes her thoughts made great sense, other times I was left wondering what she was trying to say. For example, one day she was talking about finding the inner self and described this as 'the IT, in capital letters'. Always, though, our times together were very interesting for me.

For Peggy, well, she often wondered why there were all the questions, but I think she did enjoy our 'chats'. This had not always been the case. We often did not see eye-to-eye, and indeed, could easily adopt opposing views. Sometimes these differing stances were simply part of an intellectual exercise we both enjoyed.

I discovered during my research on her life, that she was something of a closet intellectual. From the beginning of her search for spiritual knowledge she was reading the likes of the French mystic Father J.P. de Caussade and the translations of works by Thomas à Kempis and Saint Augustine. I now have these books in my library but have no temptation to pick up what I think could be quite difficult reads.

What went completely unrecognised by me during our mother-daughter talks all those years ago, was that Peggy was really telling me how she managed to cope with our family history. Although my questions to her rarely touched on the personal, her answers revealed how she thought and what worried away at her. Ever the academic, my intellectual queries would have appealed to the cerebral side of my mother. Ideas and philosophies were what interested me, and so too, Peggy.

There is one significant concept of Zen Buddhism that is particularly relevant to understanding my mother, and it was something she would constantly refer to. This is the notion of detachment or nonattachment. In layman's terms, this teaching suggests it is important to be aware of our attachment, in the main, to the activities of the mind, or our emotions. And further, by engaging in zazen or meditation, slowly the attachments wither away. Another way of putting it is, by the process of Zen practice it is possible to see through, not necessarily to eliminate, anything to which we are attached.

I have often wondered if my mother really understood the notion of attachment as it stands within Zen Buddhism. She often used to talk of living in the moment and simply dropping unwanted thoughts. She was telling me it was so easy. But then, I now know, she was well-practised at discarding feelings that disturbed her. How she handled the distressing revelation which came to me via the Reiki Master, is a significant example of how she could 'detach' herself. At the time of our talks together though, I was too enthralled by her determined religiosity to go deeper with my findings.

Through the years when we spoke of 'attachment' I would deliberately taunt her with the question of whether she thought she might have any attachment to us, her children. I always knew what she would answer, and I am almost ashamed of what I must now write. She appeared almost proud of the fact she did not feel any attachment to us. In her mind, she had reached an important milestone in Zen Buddhist practice. I now know the situation was more complicated than she was prepared to reveal, or even what she may have understood at the time. My next question to her would be, Well what about Charlie? – her dog. She would put her head in the air and refuse to answer. My response was always, "Well, we will see how detached you are when he dies." Of course, her life changed dramatically after her Charlie died.

Peggy was in the last throes of her life when she turned back to the Christian church. When I asked her the direct question of why she returned to Christianity after almost fifty years, she would usually say things such as, 'it's like going home,' or 'it's part of who I am.' This was rather an airy-fairy response for an academic mind like mine to accept, but this was often the way she saw things and it certainly stopped me from enquiring any deeper. Perhaps I am making excuses for myself because the possibility of going deeper was always there if I had wanted to delve.

One of the most telling moments in our discussions happened when we were talking about the period she spent within the High Anglican

Church in Auckland. I remember my father dropping her off at weekend retreats, where, as part of the practice of this church, she regularly attended confession. Her comment to me, that a priest told her she did not have 'dirt on her soul' because of all the confessions she had made, felt strange and out of place, but I did not investigate. I assumed the source of the dirt the priest had exonerated her from was the occasional flirtations during the neighbourhood parties. This is a standout comment if dark happenings are being looked for, but this was not my path at the time. How could it be? I did not know the full details. I had not yet gone deep inside myself to remember the more heinous matters the word dirt probably referred to.

What was important to Peggy when she turned back to the Christian church were passages from the Bible about sin and redemption. This is another pointer I ignored. I am getting annoyed with myself as I realise all this now. Although a significant element of the message of Jesus was about love, this is not what interested my mother. The doctrine of sin which involves 'the forgiving or pardoning of sin … through the death and resurrection of Jesus' would have helped erase any unease she might have had about our family history. When I was interviewing her, she would constantly repeat, "Without the crucifixion of Christ we would not have redemption." At the time I did not investigate the importance these words held for her, I simply accepted this was her concern.

Peggy often asked me why I wanted to write about her because, as she said, her life was so boring. I did not ever ask myself why on these occasions. I simply researched and asked her lots of questions as I had been trained to do. Always, my interest as I talked with her was to find the answer to the one question: Why had she returned to the Christian church?

I originally wondered how serious she was about her return to the church. Now I know so much more about her life, I think her return was very important to her. Certainly, for a while, the promises made by the church kept her stable and possibly made her feel safe. She had so much she wanted to forget. Or, had she indeed already forgotten? In her last few years, my mother's outstanding memory deserted her and sometimes she would remark about losing her mind. She was probably in the first stages of dementia. I am not going to let her off so easily and blame dementia for her ability to remove herself from the trauma in our family life. My guess is this trauma was at the core of who she had become, as it was for me. Just as she seemed unconcerned about sending me off to the Reiki lady, so it was with my writing her story – she was undaunted. Perhaps my purposeful questioning about religion ensured she never worried about where I might head with what I wrote. Did she think it was not possible to uncover her secrets? Of course, I had no idea where my interrogations would take me.

As I asked more and more questions my memory began to awaken. I made some tentative attempts to ask personal questions surrounding our family life. I cannot adequately explain, but there seemed to be something churning away at the back of my mind. There is even a faint recollection of me saying to Peggy, "Dad sexually abused me," which was accompanied by her quick and very definite denial. These first tentative memories, as a seventy-year-old, would fade in and out of my mind almost as though they were not real. At this stage, I had seen the image of my father touching me, although it was buried deep inside. Always Peggy would deny any knowledge of anything irregular in our lives together.

I did not persist in my questioning, and I wonder now, why not? Could I not confront my mother? Or was it because I was unable to unlock this door to myself for the moment? Any thoughts seemed to swirl around me unable to settle anywhere. Certainly, words were difficult to form around the subject. Dissociation seems to be in play here. This is the psychological term used when there is trauma, and the mind is unable to comprehend it and linguistically code it. It has also been explained to me how I was receiving mixed messages. Peggy is saying nothing happened. I trust her and part of me is saying "Yes, Mum must be right." Then there is the other part of me which knows but has frozen it out. Confusion seems the simplest way to describe what was happening to me at the time.

One conversation I remember having with Peggy, and it was probably around this time, was the one about my grandparents. It is interesting to me to note how sometimes small remembrances come up from the depths to help explain so much. I recall us talking about how my mother's father liked his little girl grandchildren around but not the boys, and how my father's mother was very fond of my brother, but she had no time for me. These personal revelations must have emboldened me because I asked Peggy if it was possible that Grandad could have sexually abused her. I remember asking her this question but cannot recall the context of the interrogation. I can only think now that the faint recollections I was having led me to ask the question of her. Her denial was absolute, of course. These tendencies of my grandparents and what they revealed would play out in greater detail as I learnt more.

A few months before Peggy's death something very sad happened within our family. A schism began to develop between me and my brother. His new wife did not like me. Well, she did not seem to want to associate with me. Apparently, there were various misdemeanours on my part and my brother sided with her. However, what I saw as the loss of my brother deeply affected me. As usual, Peggy seemed to take a very practical and unemotional attitude towards it. She told me it was not an uncommon thing to happen in families and we would just have to live with it. My writings a couple of years later reveal the deep hurt this event really placed on our lives. I wrote in my journal:

'Peggy told me I was strong enough and I must walk away from Douglas. At the time I did not understand why she said this. My first thought was that this must be for my brother. It would make life easier for him. Then I realised she was saying it for my benefit.'

At the time I was suffering with very sore lungs and a throat that had become almost raw from coughing fits which were so bad the muscles in my back had begun to spasm whenever I coughed. I could not talk to Douglas about how I was hurting, and my sore throat was probably a result of this lack of communication. The pain in my lungs could have been reflecting the deep sadness I felt at the developing situation. I was ill for a month, which is a very unusual occurrence for me.

This was the beginning of my realisation that our emotional state is reflected in the body. If I was so tight with emotional issues my body would let me know. The following year my heart started to flutter when I received an email from my brother which seemed to suggest he was losing his memory. For the first time ever, he had got my birthday wrong. He was wishing me happy birthday a month early. This was the first of my attacks of atrial fibrillation, which have bothered me ever since, whenever I have an emotional disturbance. My writings on my brother continued:

'My heart, my heart. What is this closeness between us – now broken?'

Then I harked back to twenty years before when I had breast cancer:

'He did not ring me – I waited for two weeks and then I rang him. All he could do was cry and cry. What is this between us?'

Our story would have a few years to play out before the question could be answered. Moreover, Peggy's advice to me to walk away from my brother is straight out of her handbook of how to handle things that are too uncomfortable.

While my health spiralled out of control, Peggy was in trouble too. Her distress at the developing split in our family took a more drastic turn. When I first learnt that my brother was distancing himself from me, I had one of those moments of knowing without knowing how. My immediate thought was *this will kill Mum*. There was absolutely nothing to suggest the truth of this rather dramatic statement which I wrote down at the time. As can often happen in these circumstances, the thinking mind quickly negated this all-knowing moment and responded back with, *don't be silly, Peggy is strong and pragmatic. Family is not important to her*, and this I also wrote down.

I now know the first intuitive thought, which I ignored, was the unconscious coming into the conscious mind. We would often talk lightly of the situation (she was always asking about the family), and we would even give a gentle smile towards each other over the words 'fancy this happening to our family'. Yet deep within my mother, there was an aching heart. This became evident to me on only one occasion, but it was a very profound moment. We were in her studio at the nursing home and were talking quite easily about what had occurred. Suddenly, I turned away with a heavy heart and gazed out the window towards the trees on the boundary line of the nursing home. When I looked back to her there was deep sadness written all over her face and a little tear dropped from her right eye. The moment was gone before I could say anything but 'that look' she gave me is one which remains with me still. This did not seem to be like the grief she had felt for the loss of her little dog, but a much deeper, inner sorrow. I felt it was a sadness of the sort that is almost unable to be acknowledged. At the time I had no understanding of what had occurred. Peggy died within two months of my seeing that look of anguish. I think she simply stopped wanting to live.

The death of my mother was easier for me to come to grips with than Jamie's. I was holding her hand as I read to her about what I had written so far about her life, and just as I came to a part mentioning her little dog, she died. She always used to say that her one big love in this life was her little Charlie, and perhaps this is emphasised in the timing of her death. This time I did not run from the scene, I stood and waited for the various protocols at the nursing home to occur. I thought at the time, *I have grown up*. Perhaps it was simply because I was not as badly affected by this death, which reminds me; when my father died, I had a distinct lack of any feeling. I find this curious now, because at the time of his death in 1990 the question of sexual abuse occurring in our family had not been raised, although I realise unconsciously it was known in my body.

Paris and Writing

After Peggy died at the age of ninety-four, I went to Paris for four months to research and write about some of what I had learnt from my mother. Again, I repeat, that is what I thought I was doing. I was very excited to be going to Paris, it was almost as though something or someone was waiting for me there. Although I had been to Paris on many occasions, often with Jamie, and with friends after he died, this time it felt quite special. There was certainly a wonderful apartment waiting for me in the Marais district. It was on the top floor of an apartment block where it looked out over the skyline of Paris and the ever-busy Rue Rambuteau. There was even a garden terrace where lavender in full flower lined the balcony. More than this, I had a gardener and a housekeeper who attended the apartment each week. I just got lucky.

Another stroke of good fortune had occurred a few years previously. I attended the opera in Paris with a couple of friends and happened to be seated next to an American lady who talked with me in detail about the American Library in the 7th arrondissement of Paris. She lived in Paris for six months of the year and worked at this library in a part-time capacity. This was the first place I turned to once I arrived in Paris. The philosophy and religious sections were a mine of information and the books I could borrow were all in English. In the middle of the public reading area, there was an enormous wooden table bordered by chairs. It was a well-used area and oozed a feeling of scholarly learning. It was like being in heaven for me – Paris and books.

In Paris, I interspersed visits from friends with my reading and writing. There was a particular three-week period I remember when I was alone. I developed a pattern over this time of going out to lunch with my little red book, often revisiting old haunts like the Carette Café in the Trocadero area. This café was quite a long walk from where I was living but I had stayed in this area with Jamie and was determined to revisit – it might give me inspiration. The café sits on a busy roundabout where the usual hustle and bustle of Paris is very much in evidence. It is a popular café and full of life. For me, the busyness only made my ponderings easier, and my concentration seemed deeper. It is interesting to read my notes from this time because, unbeknown to me, they give hints about where I really needed to go with my writing. Perhaps it was Jamie trying to jolt me into recognising the real nature of the story I had to tell. My writings were often of a spiritual nature, and this day I wrote:

'What is it I want to enquire about – find an understanding of? What is my big query about this life?'

And on I went with all my apparent spiritual ruminations. Yet reading this note now, it is obvious I was asking questions about my lived life, not the possibilities of a spiritual life.

Another time I was in my favourite brasserie, Camille, on the Rue des Francs Bourgeois in the Marais. I would often go there for a pre-dinner drink and became well-known by the staff. I must have gone there a lot because I sometimes received a free Kir Royale, a champagne cocktail I became very familiar with. It was another very lively place and I used to try and find a seat on the sidewalk terrace which looked onto the passing parade of the street.

Always when I went out, my little red book accompanied me. There was one evening when my notes once more revealed I knew there was more to my writing than simply my mother's spiritual journey. I understood I was going to write about myself, although the actual subject matter remained a mystery to me in Paris. After some seemingly spiritual meanderings I remarked, 'Is this the journey I write about alongside my mother's?' Some of these words were dismissed as irrelevant when I arrived home, others were simply misinterpreted.

What I could not do when in Paris was recall events from my childhood. I tried to do this so that I could put my mother's life into some sort of family context. Nothing would come to mind. It appeared I was there solely to seek out the knowledge to help me understand my mother's spiritual journey. I did think about my father, and all I could remember was that we were so different and had difficulty getting on. I wrote in my little red book:

'I think life with my father was not easy. I can look back and see the lack of any cerebral activity would have affected me. His was a very physical world. Lots of sport and games but no thinking. I don't know how Peggy fitted into his world. But he loved us both very much – in his way.'

There was absolutely no recollection of what had been revealed over twenty years previously.

What I did remember in Paris, and it was the only thing I could recall from my childhood, was listening to the story about the snow goose. Even now, I can see myself as a little girl, sitting on the floor engrossed in this charming tale. It was not so much the storyline I harked back to in Paris, it was the image of the snow goose flying high and free and the effect this had upon me at the time. I was in Camille and became very emotional as I brought these long-forgotten feelings back into my mind. This story had not been part of my life since I was a young girl but here it was coming up in Paris. As I sat in the café, with tears in my eyes, I wrote down what I recalled from that time when I was such a young child:

'I was transported to another world. When the story finished, I did not want to leave it. I felt an affinity with the goose. I have forgotten the storyline but still remember the feeling – I wanted to be with the goose. I think it was what the goose represented to me. This is the first time I have seriously thought about this moment in my life, but it is so real to me – as if it was yesterday.'

Once done writing I quickly gathered my things together and almost ran back to the apartment. I had to refer to the internet to obtain the complete narrative of the story, including the details about Dunkirk. It was only the flying bird I had recalled and particularly how high and easily it flew once it was nursed back to health.

I look back now and wonder why this was the only childhood memory that came to me in Paris. I understand it was the unconscious coming into the conscious mind and there is a reason for it happening at this specific time. Obviously, the comfort I felt at being in Camille is part of the explanation. I wonder, too, if the uplifting feeling I received from imagining the damaged snow goose flying high and healed was preparing me for what was to come.

When I look at my reaction to this tale now, I can see the symbolism it must have held for me, even as a little girl. A wounded bird able to get its life back on track must have been such an uplifting idea for a child who was internally damaged. As an adult in Paris, the narrative continued to touch me. I bought Paul Gallico's book and commented in my journal, 'When I read the story last night, I still had tears in my eyes when the goose entered the story.' (I must admit to the fact even now, when I review my writing, tears can arrive far too easily when the snow goose appears.)

Even though this tale had such an impact on me while I was in Paris, I did not use it in the book I later published. It did not seem to be related to anything I was writing about. It was my mother's story I was writing, not mine. Although I did not understand the importance of hearing this story, I wrote in my little red book:

'I realise this is a very meaningful event but am not sure of its symbolism for me. It is not being able to understand myself that worries me about writing my own story.'

Here I am again, thinking about writing my story but concentrating on my mother's.

In Paris, there was another bird-related memory which came to me. I recalled the many times in my childhood when I wrote, 'I would go flying far above my house and over the fields. I would go straight up.' It was usually when I was lying in bed. I seem to remember reading somewhere that imaginative flying as a child is a desire to escape one's environment. The psychological term for this escape into an inner world is again that word, dissociation. Something I have probably spent a lifetime practising. Although there was much for me to fly from it was not remembered in Paris.

Returning to the snow goose story had awakened my love of birds. The more I read the writings of great philosophers such as Schopenhauer and Jung, the deeper I went into my own spiritual world. I would go for an early morning walk through the streets of Paris and eventually end up in a little park surrounded by gardens and trees. Here I meditated to the sound of birds as they happily chirped.

Another event with birds was almost a psychotic experience. One evening at dusk I was sitting on my terrace contemplating. Suddenly I saw a flock of swallows swooping in and out through the high-rise apartments on the skyline. I was almost overcome by the sight of these beautiful birds playing in this stunning setting. It was a repeat of a scene Jamie and I had witnessed one early evening while we were visiting Assisi, a long time ago. In Italy, the swallows were flying over a valley and did not disappear and reappear as they so magically did in Paris. My reaction to seeing these swallows was rather over the top – I saw it as a sign from Jamie that I was on the right track with my writing. I was not, of course. I was writing about the wrong person.

The following evening, I looked for the swallows again and as if to say to me, 'yes, we were here,' they did arrive. This time their number was much less, and they did not return while I remained in Paris.

On my arrival home from Paris, I settled into writing out the details of my mother's spiritual journey. Having experienced my own spiritual awakening, I was in a much better position to write her story than before I left for Paris. I wrote with the help of the journal she wrote for her family, my journal of personal reflections, the little red book from Paris, all the interviews we did together, and Peggy's religious books which had now become part of my library.

Peggy's books contained written notes in longhand and shorthand (a friend translated for me) and she had underlined many sentences and words. Her books revealed so much which at the time I simply put down to her spiritual journey. After all, this is what I was writing about (I am making excuses for myself here).

Using all these sources, I wrote a portrait of her life that was more hagiography than a true account. I admired her apparently deep spirituality and wrote with this in mind. Let me also say I was persuaded by my mother's own account of her spiritual life in her journal. Yet, I remind myself, all the words she underlined in her books – and there was an enormous amount of underlining – identify her personal concerns which I completely ignored at the time.

Her Zen books were particularly very revealing. She has underlined phrases such as 'It's the play of our minds … that is the problem' and 'Every memory we stick to devastates our life.' I saw these words underlined and used them to explain her quest for the 'silent mind'. There was no thought on my part to investigate these important words, and others like them, and look at them from a more personal aspect. It never entered my mind to ask what was going on for my mother in her life and why exactly was she searching so hard for the 'silent mind'. Yet, at the end of one of the chapters of my writing, I wrote, 'I am still left wondering if she ever found what she was searching for.' There was a hesitancy on my part and quite rightly so, yet I had no way of knowing at this stage what else could be involved. I have been reminded again and again as I work my way through this story, it is only when we are ready to see something that it is revealed.

There is another way to explain this complete ignorance I displayed while writing my mother's story. I was an academic who could make an argument out of anything. I remember how delighted I was to learn during my first year of studying history at Sydney University, there could be more than one way to answer an historical question. My friends can testify to my having the unfortunate knack of arguing without substantial knowledge. It is amazing for me to see now how I made an argument about my mother seem sensible from an incorrect premise. I used the idea of reincarnation to argue my mother's strong leaning towards the Christian church was probably a result of past life experiences as a nun or monk. Well, it was her past life – within our family – which was instrumental in turning her back to the church. The argument I should have been making was that she went back to the church because it promised to forgive her.

On her involvement with Zen Buddhism, I paid attention to her interest in the notion of detachment as the means to help her achieve her aim of the silent mind. I should have been arguing that as a Zen Buddhist, she was encouraged to drop all unwanted thoughts. The concepts of both reincarnation and detachment would have helped my mother to navigate her way through life relatively unscathed by our family history. My only excuse for the academic subtleties I used to exonerate her at the time is, I did not know enough.

Once I had completed the first draft of my mother's story, I gave it to a friend to read. He is a deeply spiritual man and knew my mother, although not well. He pointed out what I had done – I had set my mother up to be a representation of spiritual perfection when she was really nothing of the sort. My friend explained, her spiritual journey had been one of understanding with her intellect only. Furthermore, he suggested her spiritual ego was quite monstrous. While I was interviewing her the suggestion of this ego came out at times, particularly when she compared her own spirituality with mine. I do not think I ever thought of myself as a spiritual person, but she would often see me in negative terms compared to her own deep spirituality. My friend's comment, "It feels like you are being put down by her all the time," explains my mother's mindset. I knew she was jealous of my university education and perhaps this example of spiritual arrogance was her way of feeling better about herself. A significant observation from my friend was seen in his question, "Was she ever truly honest with herself?" He knew nothing of her past, but his question raised the central issue of her life.

Eventually, I accepted what I called her false spirituality and after much anguish rewrote my mother's story. It was only a half-hearted attempt because I was unable to fully denounce her as a spiritual fraud. The extent to which I did drop the notion of her deep spirituality left me feeling distressed and almost guilty. For some reason I so wanted her journey to be a good one. Perhaps I already knew her life was not what I imagined, or indeed what she had projected.

I look at my journal writings around the time I was completing the book and see there is an enormous outpouring of emotion. There was so much pain around my writing, and it was primarily about my having to denounce my mother's own sense of her deep spirituality. I wrote:

> 'I am crying for what I have to do – be honest about my mother's journey – a fool's paradise has come to my mind … such destruction. Such pain and suffering again – for Peggy. Why be so concerned for her who was less than kind to me?'

I read these words now and realise there was much more going on for me than calling my mother's spiritual life into disrepute. Further on in this note to myself are the words:

> 'What is the truth, Mama? What really is it about – I know, I know: Simply feel it – something you were unable to do. What a journey I have put myself on – where will it end?'

There are also numerous writings from this time in which I try to deal with a 'heartbreak' which could not be understood. 'A desperate sadness' was one of the phrases I used to describe my state. It was as though there was some inner tumult taking place inside me. This period was so very difficult for me I wonder now if the writing of my mother's story began to break down a resistance within me. Unbeknown to me, the struggle to contain my history was beginning to fracture. My emotional outbursts were only the beginning. Deep down I knew there were much more distressing events to be detailed, yet the time was obviously not right for me to write them out, let alone remember them.

My mother's story was published, although slowly over the following few months I began to feel uneasy about what I had written. Something was not right. At the time there was no way I could explain this feeling as it slowly developed. I can now see I knew deep inside myself this was not a true account of my mother's life. It was a whitewash of what her life had been. I did not want to promote the book or even give it to friends. Those who did read it usually commented on the coldness and the selfishness of my mother. I did not deliberately set out to portray her in this way but her strident purposefulness in the pursuit of spiritual illumination, above all else, made these traits so obvious. I did not investigate the apparent coolness or her self-centred attitude. It was not what I was writing about.

Then I reread her diary and paid attention to her reminisces about her family. There I thought I saw a mother and grandmother who had been unable to show the deep love she felt. Was her coldness only superficial? It was, again, a very emotional time for me because, on this reading of her diary, I saw the suffering she had experienced throughout her life. I remembered that look of deep sadness when we were talking about the breakdown in the relationship with my brother, Douglas, and I assumed a connection between that look and her feelings for her family.

Ever the academic I mounted an intellectual argument about what that look meant and what her words suggested she felt for her children and grandchildren. Another chapter, 'In Hindsight', was added to the story, although not once did I raise any personal questions in the effort to help explain her long spiritual journey. Of course, the image of me as a child being touched by my father, as Peggy looked on, was firmly buried within me.

The breakdown in the relationship between Douglas and myself was so significant to my mother, it suggested I delve further. That look required an explanation. It told of such a deep sadness. Yet she was so not a family person. Easily able to let her children go their own way, there was no emotional holding on to us as we grew up and left home. Also, when she came to Australia, she was able to leave behind in New Zealand, without any qualms, the sister she had spent so much pleasure time with during their later years. There were no apparent great regrets around the loss of any family relationships. Despite this, she writes at the time my brother and his family were leaving Auckland, how much she will miss them and then says, 'I love you all, more than I can say.' What else do I require from her? Her journal makes it clear about her love of family. My feelings, though, suggest her actions tell us more than the words she wrote.

Parts of what I wrote at this time show a picture of my mother as she struggled with life within our family. Her mantra about us being here on this planet to learn and mature as human beings was very relevant to her life. She certainly learnt a lot from the many trials and tribulations she went through on her spiritual search. At a personal level, she still had to learn about and experience the feeling of deep, compassionate human love. Peggy wrote in her journal about her failings as a mother and grandmother. She loved us as babies but did not seem able to cope as we got older, she told us. Before she died though, I wrote she was able to feel the love a mother can have for her children. The basis of my argument for this chapter of my mother's life reasoned that she felt this deep love when she realised the bonds holding her family together were being broken.

During our lives, my brother and I rarely saw any demonstration of love from our mother. Yet in her last year while at the nursing home, I remember observing her shining eyes when she was with us on the odd occasion. There were a couple of times when the three of us were able to meet up for lunch at a restaurant, and on these occasions, she had a special glow in her eyes. She was so happy, just being in the moment with her two children and those shining eyes were noticeable only when the three of us were together. She did love us.

My argument maintained it was as she saw the ties of family being broken between myself and Douglas, she experienced the love for her children she had previously only written about in her journal a decade ago. Family bonds held no place for Peggy during her years of spiritual searching. It was in the last months of her life that she came upon this lesson of life on our planet – she learnt about unconditional love for family. When my brother's and my first marriages broke up, Peggy was unaffected by the turn of events. She remained equable and objective. There was never any taking the side of her children, as is so often the case in these matters. Yet on this occasion of a breakdown in relations between her two children, it was deeply felt – that look of desolation was very disturbing to witness.

How do I explain this anguish felt by my mother? A book written by Jean-Yves Leloup helped me understand. He suggests there is a thin line between sentimental love and emotional attachment and that of distance and indifference, and one of the lessons of this life is to learn to tread along the middle path of compassionate love. He states, 'Our purpose on earth is to learn to love truly,' and even more, he notes, 'It is my belief that we spend our entire lives learning this.' These words seem so appropriate to understanding Peggy and her learning of this last lesson. Her tendency was to appear indifferent towards her family, yet in her last weeks, I think she learnt about Leloup's middle way. She dropped her apparent coolness and felt a love borne out of concern for her two children. The expression of her love at this time did not have anything to do with her need to love or be loved but with her compassionate love for her children and, my guess is, a deep concern for how we would handle this unexpected family ordeal. At long last, she had become a normal, loving mother.

Then there is the period of her last few months at the nursing home where she connected with a man also staying at the home. I believe this man became the means for my mother to feel unconditional love for a man before she died. It was difficult for me to write of this for a long time because I did not know what to make of the situation and it seemed too close and personal for Peggy and the man involved.

When she arrived at the nursing home, this man, whose name I did not know but will call him Vincent, was virtually catatonic. He would sit in the dining room with his eyes closed and not move. He seemed literally dead to the world. Eventually, I found out that his wife, who had been living with him in the home, had died. Peggy did not know this. On seeing Vincent, Peggy began to bend over him and give him a little peck on his forehead. There was no response from him, but I am sure she did this whenever she saw him sitting motionless. She certainly planted that little kiss on his forehead every time she saw him when I was with her, even though kissing people was something she avoided doing for most of her life. I am convinced this small act directed towards Vincent was one of compassion on the part of Peggy. I understood it as her saying to him, 'don't worry, it will be all right'. Perhaps that coldness disappeared during her last year of life.

After a few months, Vincent slowly began to awaken to the world. During the Christmas period of 2013, I saw him talking with two young adults, who at the time I thought were perhaps his grandchildren. I do not know what sort of interaction occurred between Peggy and Vincent once he 'woke up'. I did ask the nursing staff about him and was told he had deep dementia.

It was Vincent who I consider showed unconditional love to my mother. I do not remember exactly how long it was between when he woke up and Peggy dying, but it was possibly only a few months. What I did see and remember very clearly was the connection between these two old persons just ten days before Peggy passed away.

My mother had stopped eating properly. Any encouragement from me to get her to eat more did not seem to have any effect. The kitchen staff at the nursing home must have been having the same problem. I think they hatched a plan to try and get her to eat. The plan involved sitting her with Vincent in the dining room. Previously she had been sitting with a group of women but on this night, I saw one of the staff place Peggy next to Vincent, who was sitting around a table with a couple of other men. Perhaps the staff thought it would relax her – I do not know – but this was the scene for me to experience another of those moments with my mother that is etched in my mind. As I was about to leave her at the dining table, she introduced me to Vincent. He was not interested in looking at me because he only had eyes for Peggy. And what a look it was. It seemed to be a look of the sort I can only imagine pure love would look like. It was open and almost childlike in its innocence, and so of the moment. It was a vision I will not forget, and it still brings tears to my eyes if I think about it.

The look on my mother's face was also something to be observed. Her eyes were light and sparkling as though she was in the first flush of young love. I do not know what part dementia played in this exchange, but I realise there were no thoughts, no filters, and simply a living in the moment as these two old people sat down beside each other – and connected so beautifully.

The bond between these two was further in evidence on the day Peggy died. As I was waiting outside my mother's room for the nursing home sister to officially declare Peggy had died, I saw Vincent, too far in the distance for me to see his face, but I could feel his agitation as he stood at his doorway looking down towards my mother's room. Somehow, I now realise, he knew she had died. It was the only time I saw him in the corridors of the nursing home.

This story of love now delights me to share it. Something went right for my mother at last. I am crying for the sheer pleasure of remembering it.

Tapping into the Past

My writing about Peggy and familial love was based in academic nuances and demonstrates just how far I had to go before not only understanding my mother's life but my own too. I still had absolutely no idea where I was heading. There was no real perception of my being on a personal journey of my own. As I keep repeating, it is only when we are ready that realisation happens. And in my case, it came slowly, slowly. I wonder now why it was so slow. Was it the nature of what had to be revealed? Or were there some inadequacies on my part? I can look back and be thankful for the snail's-pace. Perhaps I could have been overwhelmed if too much had arrived at my door all at once.

Suddenly, as if from nowhere, depression became my companion. I had never suffered from depression before and now, over a nine-month period, I would walk into my garden feeling such despair. Although there were numerous pathways under large camellia trees, ponds with running water and places such as the arbour to sit and contemplate, there was now no joy for me in these beautiful surroundings I had designed with such love over many years. My garden no longer gave me the comfort and support it had generated for so long. Instead, feelings of dread would well up, only for me to force them down and go on with my life. The words *oh no, oh no* also came into my mind at this time. I had no idea what was happening to me.

For a few years, it had been quite harrowing as I examined my mother's words. On the few occasions when I read between the lines of her writing I would end up in tears. I assumed the depression I was experiencing was a hangover from the writing and rewriting I had been engaged in, for perhaps too many years.

Then I went to Auckland, my home town, for a holiday. Here, that unknown guide stepped in. I was visiting with a group of girlfriends, and we had all sorts of adventures planned, certainly for the first week. For me, though, there were other unknown plans underway. My heart was in a little bit of trouble – I think it could have been warning me of what was to come. In Auckland, I had not become conscious of the personal insight about my heart and emotional troubles. The only thing I can recall is the various tests carried out and then the doctor told me I could go. I would be all right and could join my friends. This was not part of the unknown plan.

On the way back to the apartment, I twisted my ankle so badly I literally could not move it. This stopped me. I did not want to worry my friends about buying me books to read so the only thing for me to do in these circumstances was to start writing. I sat on the balcony of my apartment overlooking Auckland Harbour, with my foot propped up on a cushion, and began to write in longhand.

Whether it was the home setting of Auckland City or the special touch of personal handwriting, the past came rumbling back to me. Whereas in Paris I could remember very little about my life, here it came back to me in enormous sweeps. My father was the main source of the memories that swept back. All his sexual misdemeanours: the many and various encounters he had with women and young girls which I was privy to rose to the surface of my mind. Also, the image of my father touching me as my mother looked on reappeared. This time, everything I recollected was written down. It could never be buried again. My recall of how I handled these revelations is hazy; my guess is that my ability to disengage emotionally came in handy once more.

I arrived back in Australia with all my scribblings (this is what I saw them as) and put them away in a drawer in my study. The time was obviously not right for me to reach any deeper. Enough had been summoned up for the moment and it could not be forgotten again. That is what I thought.

The depression gathered pace and those dreaded words *oh no, oh no*, became stronger. This time the only way I could reduce my anxiety was to walk around and around my terrace garden, then sit down at one of the outdoor chairs, and then get up and walk around again. Even the gentle flow of water from the fountain in my garden pond could not calm my agitation. There was a feeling within me I had to take some action regarding my situation, but I felt frightened. What was it that had me so fearful? The strength of my despair suggested something very unpleasant. It was almost as though there was some horror about to surface from within me.

I gathered myself together and went off to a counsellor. I understood there was a need to write out whatever was worrying away at me but this time I was very reluctant to put pen to paper. I do not think I wanted to face whatever it was, and at this stage, I had no comprehension of what it could be. It seemed to be something rather ugly and even menacing.

The notes about my father had been filed away in my study and were virtually erased from a mind that found comfort in forgetting.

My whole demeanour was one of panic and anxiety, and the counsellor picked this up. As I sat down in her quite sparse room with only one table and two chairs, she looked straight into my eyes and said, "Well, you needed to come and see me, didn't you."

My one question to her was my concern about writing out what was worrying away at me. Did I really need to do it? This was all I wanted to know. Inside myself I recognised my anguish was about me and my history, but anything definite still evaded me. I had no idea exactly what my despair was about or what it was suggesting.

The counsellor convinced me to write out what was worrying away at me, although I cannot recall what argument she used to persuade me. I really did know what I had to do, but there was the faint hope I did not need to go there. She probably used calming words like, 'it will make you feel much better once you've written it out'. The counsellor won me over and without any further torment, I went home to write.

My notes from Auckland came out of the drawer and I began to write the final chapter of my mother's life. At least that had been my intention. What developed was a body of writing primarily about my father, with questions arising, unprompted, about the propriety of my mother. I revisited 'that look' she gave me when we were together in her studio and realised how deeply she was disturbed by our early family life. I am still unsure about her tears which fell at the time. Were they about grief or guilt over not doing something about the situation within our family? Perhaps both. As I reread my early notes, I see that I knew so much I was not prepared to face. I wrote then:

'My mother's life was a lie, and she knew it – this is why her tears were in that moment.'

A year after I had written of my mother's love for her children, I put together the following details. At the time I thought I was at long last coming to the end of my writing, hence the title 'Finally'. Although I have learnt much more since writing this, it is a true account of how I saw the circumstances at the time.

Finally

Throughout the book written about my mother, the question uppermost in my mind was why she returned to the Christian church. I did not consider asking why she went on such a strident and seemingly purposeful spiritual search. That question is central to what I now write about. I wonder if my mother's story is more complicated than I have previously viewed it. I need to go a little deeper, and for this, I will look within our family. This is an area I have not written about because I did not see it as being related to my mother's spiritual journey. Now, quite definitely I see there could be a very strong connection between the two. Moreover, at this moment as I begin to write again, I have no idea where this exercise is going to lead me, although I realise certain unhappy truths about my family life will need to be exposed.

The memories of family life that came flooding back while I was in Auckland revolved around my father. A big memory was the one about Sunday mornings. Sunday was an important day in the social life of our family, but particularly for my father. He used to go off on a Sunday morning on the pretext he was going to see about work. I suspect he was often out on another sort of business that would include drinking, although I have nothing to back up this statement. I know he would turn up at the house of my cousin Penny on a Sunday looking for something to drink, and I am sure there were other friends he could call on.

Peggy must have questioned what he was up to because she nurtured his sweet tooth by baking beautiful cookies and cakes which I think she hoped would help to keep him at home on a Sunday morning. If she did not do the baking or get it done in time he could be out for the whole morning.

At other times my mother would organise a picnic lunch to take to the beach, when she would bake, for my father, his favourite bacon and egg pie. I do not remember my father being particularly engaged in our picnics. There was almost a disinterest, as though he wanted to be somewhere else. He was always looking at his watch and ready to leave early. Sunday was his playtime, although I am still not sure what he played at. What I do know for certain, is that drink would have been involved. Was it his need for a drink or something else that made him almost agitated?

Another more favourable memory of my father was his love of music, with Frank Sinatra and Ella Fitzgerald being his favourite singers. Their records were often played when my father was in a light mood during the weekend. His love of music is seen in the quite extensive selection of long-playing records we had in a period when playing records was something quite new in New Zealand.

He enjoyed all sorts of dancing and was very good at it – he seemed to have a natural rhythm. I realise now that in their later years my mother's refusal to go to gatherings with him where there was dancing, was possibly because of his wandering eyes and probably hands. I remember one time overhearing her talking to him in an almost disgusted tone about his behaviour the previous evening.

The alcohol is something I cannot forget. Whether it was workmates or neighbours, all were welcome at our house to drink with my father. His constant drinking and chasing after women is emphasised in a story told to me recently by one of my cousins.

We were all away together for our annual camping holiday. Apparently, my father had been away somewhere for a long time, and either my mother knew where he was or found out. She bundled the four of us children into the car and drove around to a nearby house where there were all sorts of games going on, involving cards, women, and alcohol. Peggy grabbed my father, pulled him outside and threw him into the car with us children looking on open-mouthed. I do not remember this incident although, I was told, I did not talk to my father for the rest of the holiday.

There were other occasions through the years when my father allowed his proclivity for sexual abnormality to take hold of him. He touched young teenage girls. I personally know of two incidents and a third I heard from Peggy. My guess is, there were many more. The episode my mother spoke of resulted in the girl, a distant cousin, telling him he was a 'dirty old man'. The girl was a mid-teenager and was old enough to stand up to him. I suspect, though, he was untouched by the derogatory term she threw at him.

I think back to the time my mother told me this story and wonder what was going on in our minds. We did not ever discuss exactly what he was accused of doing. Did we accept this outrageous behaviour? It was another time, another place. It was no more acceptable then than it is now and yet these men, and I suspect there were many of them, got away with it.

I was reminded while I was socialising in Auckland, of the two occasions my father allowed his repugnant actions to come to the fore within my circle. I was having lunch with a girlfriend from my early school years and was telling her of the memories I was having in relation to my father. She hesitated before she said, "There's something I've never told you."

My heart sank, I knew what was coming. And sure enough, she told me of the time she was staying at our house for a three-month period while her parents were overseas, and my father was on the lawn teaching her how to swing a golf club. Yes – it is obvious. She thought he touched her on the breast, but it happened so quickly and deftly she questioned herself. She then said to me, "But I know he did touch me."

In a strange coincidence, that night I had arranged to go out with another cousin who I knew had been touched by my father. When this cousin got married my father had not been invited to the wedding even though he was from her side of the family and an uncle. I had wondered to my mother why they had not been invited – my brother, Douglas, and his wife had received an invitation. Peggy hinted at an incident in the past when my father had sexually misbehaved. I had never talked with my cousin about this unpleasant episode in her life.

On the night we met up for dinner, the shock of hearing my girlfriend's story had subdued me to the extent it was quite noticeable. My cousin asked me what was wrong and out it poured. She looked at me in dismay. Apparently, the same thing had happened for her, when my father touched the top of her inner leg as she sat beside the swimming pool, aged about eleven – she also wondered whether it had really occurred, but she knew it had. The awful part of these stories is it sounds as though he was well-practised.

Once he was almost caught out in one of his sordid practices. My recollection is rather vague because I was living in London at the time. He made the mistake of talking dirty over the telephone to a neighbour's teenage daughter, who lived across the road from my parent's house. Apparently, he made some comment about being able to see her in her underwear at night. The girl recognised his voice but, somehow, he managed to squirm out of having to take responsibility for his grubby ways.

These sexual encounters were further highlighted when my mother, who worked as the secretary to the local police station, told one of the local policemen who she was married to. Peggy told me the policeman was horrified. Possibly the local police officers knew more about my father than his family did. Certainly, they would have been fully aware of his drinking habits and the danger he was on the road. My guess is they also knew about his sexual offences.

My own experience of watching my father engage with young women occurred when I was in my late twenties. There were two most unpleasant experiences while I was on holiday in Europe with my parents and then-husband, Bill. It happened while we were seated at a restaurant. What my father would do was look for an attractive young woman who was facing him across the room of the restaurant and then he would concentrate his attention upon her. Eventually, the girl would feel his gaze and look at him. This must have been the thrill he was seeking because from that moment nothing else existed for him. If we had got up and left him sitting at the table alone, I do not think he would have noticed, he was so engrossed in whatever, and wherever he was in that moment. It was as though he was in another world.

Recently I read about Oscar Wilde, the nineteenth-century writer, who displayed a 'chilly emotional solipsism' (where self is the only thing that exists) when he fell for the poet Lord Alfred Douglas. This sounds like an apt description of my father when in pursuit of women and girls. Perhaps it is a suitable expression to apply to all sexual predators.

One of the two occasions when I saw my father engaged in this steely intent was in Paris, and it almost ended in a fight with the young girl's partner. We were seated quite comfortably at the end of our meal when suddenly the three of us, Bill, Mum, and I, realised something was not right. There was a commotion on the other side of the restaurant. I looked across to my father and realised what was happening.

We paid for our meal and quickly hustled my father out of the restaurant. There was no shame on his part, only an annoyance that we had interrupted his bad behaviour.

I am left wondering what he thought he was doing. Did he imagine the girls were flirting with him? Or was he simply fantasising?

In Auckland, when I began to remember these incidents, I wrote in big capital letters, MY FATHER WAS A SLEAZE. He was more than this. He demonstrated a deep sexual perversion.

What also occurred in these restaurant confrontations was the reappearance of that look on my father's face. At this stage of my life, the leer I had seen as I lay in my cot had not been remembered. Now, on my much older father, I observed this unpleasant look. He was in his late fifties and by now was beginning to look slightly dissipated. His drinking was taking its toll on his good looks. I suspect the look I observed in the restaurant encounters appeared whenever he engaged in his sordid behaviour. That look said so much. Whether it was a sneer, an ogle, or simply a smirk, it spoke of a well-practised immorality. It told of an unscrupulous individual out for only his own satisfaction. This was my father.

How was my mother able to handle all these atrocities? Put simply, I think she buried them somewhere deep inside herself and sought solace through her spiritual journey. Or was it an escape she was looking for? That is, after 1955 – how she coped up until this time I cannot imagine. Her crushing of the whisky glass I witnessed as a small girl suggests her state of mind.

When I was in Auckland with those early memories resurfacing and I recalled the image of my father touching me while my mother looked on, I wrote, 'Oh Peggy, where was your moral fibre? Your daughter and you knew.' Yet, I give myself a cautionary warning and tell myself there could be parts of my mother's life I do not know about and perhaps she requires the understanding from me she was unable to give.

I knew Peggy was deeply troubled in her marriage, but she did not seem able to break with my father. She was a good-looking woman and remained so for the rest of her life. Through the years she had admirers. I remember when I was in my mid-teens telling her she was not to leave my father. The cheek of me. I cannot imagine why I would suggest such a thing when I had such difficulties getting on with him myself as a teenager. A psychologist would be able to explain this anomaly. At the time I knew my mother had received a bottle of perfume from a man she worked with. She would have been involved in the Christian church around this period – the relationship came to an end, although the details are not clear to me now.

Another time, in the late 1980s, when I was visiting my parents from Sydney, Peggy confessed to me she wanted to walk out into the sea at Piha (her favourite swimming spot) and just keep walking. I remember how she looked at the time – pale and ill. I think my father had been on one of his drinking binges when he would arrive home late and very much under the weather. Even at this time, as an adult, I could not help her by trying to talk it through with her. These were things we simply did not discuss.

Her choice not to leave him was, to a certain extent, due to the financial stability he provided. She once told me she did not want to walk away from all they had gathered around them (in material terms). She knew her man and understood there would be another woman in his life very quickly. She said she did not want another woman taking what was rightfully hers.

In recent months I have had a strong feeling I had still not completed my mother's story, even though I had analysed what I thought that sad look was about. Now I am asking why she went on such a long spiritual journey

I am beginning to understand my own ineptitude at being objective regarding my family. For instance, my attempt to make my mother softer and less controlled was probably because this is what I wanted from her. So too, my desire to have her love us with the unconditional love I imagine most mothers give their children. Perhaps I have always wanted to make things pleasant as a reaction to my childhood.

The depression I have suffered from in recent months is still with me. The words 'oh no, oh no' come up from my unconscious and I push them away as I walk round and round my terrace garden. The feeling that comes with the words is too ghastly for me to face. I must try to find out what this emotion is telling me. It could hold the clue to Peggy's long spiritual journey and that look of such sadness.

It is strange to me, although I really knew I was writing about myself, my concern at this time was still about telling my mother's story. I continued writing:

'I have finished putting into the computer the things I needed to remember about my background. Today instead of typing I am writing out in longhand.'

Whenever I put pen to paper I would do so in my conservatory where there was a big bronze Buddha in one corner, and three walls of large glass doors looking out over my extensive garden where the bower birds would swoop in and out at dusk. The atmosphere was one of complete serenity. There was a small raffia desk, belonging to my mother, along one of the glass walls, and here I would sit contemplating and composing at the same time. I cannot emphasise enough how comfortable this place felt for me – it was my Buddha Room.

I carried on with my handwriting.

'I have reached the moment where I must go deep within and ask questions of myself. What is the deep pain which comes up when I cry out, 'oh no, oh no'? It is connected to the so sad look from my mother, and it is something to do with her two children. What went on, K?'

There was then much meandering on paper about the relationship with my brother; my hurts and fears in relation to him. Then I asked the question:

'What is this between us? I thought I looked out for him so as to keep my father away from doing sexual damage to him.'

I have no idea where this thought came from – it arrived unheralded out of nowhere. The unconscious? While I was in this almost mystical atmosphere of my Buddha Room, I suddenly remembered the special exercise I had been taught a few years after Jamie had died.

The grief counsellor who helped me process my grief over the loss of my husband told me of a procedure I could use if I was ever in a quandary about something. I think he also thought it could help me make spiritual contact with Jamie if needed. He told me to recognise very definitely what it was I wanted to know and when the question was formed it had to be very exact. It had to be simple and straightforward with no 'ifs and buts'. Then, I was to put myself into a deep meditation, place my hands on my knees and tap them alternatively for about a minute while I asked the question. As a result, the answer would present itself in picture form.

I am sure this procedure is meant to be used for serious life questions only. However, I remember a few years ago worrying about a commercial property I wanted to sell, although I was not sure if the roof required expensive repairs. The counsellor's procedure came out of the closet for the first time. I tapped my knees and asked the question about whether it would sell even if I did not investigate doing the repairs. The picture that presented itself was of my building with both a grey roof and a shiny new one and a real estate agent's board outside with the 'Sold' sign on it. Whether I did the work or not, it was going to sell. Obviously, if I had replaced the roof, I would have received more money for my building, but I stopped worrying and after a few months it sold. I have not returned to this exercise since then.

Now I had remembered the procedure there was no hesitation on my part to use it again. Once into meditation I began to tap my knees and asked the question, What was going on under the veneer of our family life? This question arrived without thought or premeditation. My guess is it came from my unconscious and arose out of the spiritual atmosphere created in my Buddha Room.

Slowly and surely a grainy picture emerged of naked bodies in a double bed. There were two adults and two little children who frolicked about between the bedclothes. The faces and bodies were shadowy and unrecognisable, although the bedroom furniture was well-defined, indeed, crystal clear. It was my parent's built-in bed with the bookshelves over the top and beside the bed were the matching side tables. There was no mistaking the furniture.

Although on first appearance this picture was almost light-hearted, the feeling I had and the words I wrote out told a completely different story. A feeling of horror and deep dread crept over me. I got up from the chair and went to my pen and paper and wrote:

> 'Group sex – family sex on a Sunday morning when we were very young children.'

I continued:

'Oh no, oh no – my body tells me it is so. I am in tears – I need confirmation of this. I need help to process this.'

My body was virtually shaking with the shock of the words I wrote down and today I find it difficult to imagine the composure required to write out those words so clearly. If they had not been written down though, I could quite easily have thought I had imagined such a revelation. There was no way for me to escape these words.

Once finished writing, I ran through the hallway, grabbed my car keys from the hall table and hurried downstairs to the car. I remember burning up my driveway on the way to find help. I knew where I was heading, because as if by accident, a few days previously I had walked into a shop looking for some herbal essence. The shop was well hidden and previously I had not known of its existence. It is no longer there. The atmosphere was one of deep calmness. Instinctively I asked the proprietor of the shop if she knew of anyone who could help me access repressed memory. I did not think I could do it by myself. It was this shop I returned to for assistance.

The proprietor made a phone call and at very short notice a lovely lady helped me understand these events in my life. She was there for me. Her room was very colourful and peaceful at the same time. There were low soft chairs and cushions scattered throughout. Some of the understanding I wrote about at this time was because of her two-hour session with me. I came away, not with the horror I went in with, but relief that the dreaded had finally come out.

My lovely lady helped me understand my lack of victimhood. In recent years the sexual abuse cases that have come before the public eye have always promoted the idea sexual abuse leaves victims in its wake. Well, we are victims of sexual abuse, but we do not necessarily have to sign up for victimhood. I do not feel as though I am a casualty of sexual abuse, yet I do remember when I was in my twenties calling myself 'second-hand goods', much to the shock of those hearing my words. Twenty years before the Reiki sessions brought the sexual abuse back into my consciousness my body knew about it, of course. My lady told me I was lucky because I had heard the snow goose story. As a young girl, there was a recognition by me that the damaged goose was able to be healed. Deep in my being, almost as though it was in my DNA, I understood if the goose could be healed, so could I. There was no need for me to be damaged for the rest of my life. Perhaps what helped in this process was the fact there was not a lot of time between the start of the abuse and my hearing the story that so affected me. Thus, the luck entailed here. This does not mean I was unaffected by what happened to me. There have been significant unhappy consequences, some of which are still in play today.

The acceptance of my ability to heal, like the snow goose, came out in another way when I had breast cancer. Although the cancer was caught early, it was multi-faceted – there were not just one or two lumps. It meant the cancer cells could be anywhere in my breast. The surgeons wanted to cut my breast off – one of them wanted to take both off – others in the medical profession wanted to either burn or poison the cells out of my body. The sense of my own ability to heal myself was so strong and confident at the time, I stood firm against the medical advice, although I did take the hormone-related drug Tamoxifen for four and a half years. Practitioners in the field of alternative medicine were also very supportive of me. Only now do I realise the basis of the confidence I had in myself to heal at the time. Still today, the story of the goose brings tears to my eyes.

There is no need for me to go into more explicit detail about these Sunday 'frolics'. It must be stated though, this was not innocent fun.

The reaction of my body, plus the pending dread I had felt over several months, strongly suggests the horror of what was going on during these Sunday mornings. There was sexual excitement in that bed, certainly for my father. What about my mother? Did she go along with it because she was unable to say no? Did my father have some hold over her? Did she justify this predatory behaviour in some way to herself? These questions will probably never be answered. There is enough to know already.

Of course, our Sunday mornings changed over time. As we got older, I remember my brother and I took turns making our parents breakfast and taking it to them while still in bed, and we delighted in doing so. The sexual atmosphere my words had conjured up must have disappeared because I do not have any bad feelings around taking breakfast to them in the bedroom. It might be a case of me not wanting to dig any further. Yet the fact I remember myself often pretending to be a ballerina, dancing in the lounge to music playing on a Sunday morning radio programme, indicates a more carefree child, not one who is distressed.

How do I feel about my mother now? Since arriving back from Auckland, I have felt both sad for her and slightly angry with her. Now I realise that something held her back from being able to look after her little girl properly. My feelings are only of sorrow that she could not overcome whatever it was.

My mother's plight can be uncovered by what her body tells us. Throughout my childhood, she had very bad dermatitis, particularly on her hands and arms. I remember one time the doctor coming to our house in the middle of the night to give her an injection to relieve the itch because it was so bad. My books on what the body shows you about your emotions suggest Peggy's skin condition demonstrated how angry she was. The dermatitis continued to flare up throughout her life which implies she was never able to come to terms with what happened in her life.

Another characteristic of my mother provides a further hint of her emotional troubles. Throughout her life, she suffered from a little cough, something my father almost got annoyed with her about at times. It sounded like a little tickle which with some control could be stopped, but she was never able to curb it. My books indicate any chest problem, such as this cough, is about the protection of our deepest secrets and emotions. I must confess on the odd occasion when I have been deep into the telling of my story, I hear my mother's little cough coming up from within me.

Then there is my brother. I cannot write about how he may or may not have been affected by our Sunday mornings. He was three years younger than me and would have been a tiny little boy. Perhaps he was too young to be left affected as I was. He once said to me that he was glad he did not have any female children because of our father, so he certainly knew about our father's sexual tendencies. I am no longer in touch with my brother and talking with him about these revelations is not the way to renew our relationship. My feeling of deep grief at the diminished relationship between us suggests the bond we had once. Is it because those Sunday mornings connected us in some special way? I can imagine myself trying to 'please my daddy' so he would keep away from my little brother. However, this is only within my imagination, I have no details to back up this idea and do not want to delve any deeper.

Before I tapped into the horror of my early life, I had raised some questions in my mind about that look of deep sadness from my mother. I wondered, did she in that moment realise just what her life had been? Further, I asked myself, was there something in our family life I had blanked out because it was so painful? Was there something my mother spent all those years trying to forget and escape from to finally come face to face with it again in her last months? Was this what that look was about?

And was this part of why she took this long and ultimately unsatisfactory spiritual journey? All these questions can now be answered with a firm 'yes'.

While I have since ventured further into my psyche, this is what I thought and wrote in 2017. I could never have imagined where the writing of this last chapter of my mother's story would lead. Yes, it was her story I was still writing. It is almost incomprehensible that a narrative about a seemingly deep spiritual journey could end in a tale of familial sexual abuse. I thought I now understood what had happened in our family and was relieved the fear I had lived with for months was at last explained. I could get on with my life. What a mistake. I had hardly touched on the significance of these events and what they meant to me. I was still hiding.

With hindsight, I realise I saw the picture of bodies in the double bed, but the blurred figures helped me to mentally screen what was happening. I was later to call this bedroom scene in the screenplay a 'romp', as though my brother and I were simply playing with our parents. It is evident there is almost a disconnection between the image which seemed to appear and the words I wrote out in such despair. This has been explained to me as something that can happen when a memory is too much for an individual. In psychological terms, this is when thoughts and actions become split or, again that word, disassociated. At the time I did not understand what I had experienced in my Buddha Room did not make sense. I read the words I wrote, acknowledged the sexual abuse without any comprehension of it, and retreated inside myself. Unbeknown to me the significance of this fragmentation lay in ambush waiting for me.

A few years later, I recognised it was these Sunday mornings my cousin Penny knew about. During one of their drinking occasions, my father had obviously said something to her. I have no idea what it was she understood about these mornings. There is an idea in my head that he got around the abhorrent nature of what was involved by suggesting he was teaching me and my brother about sex. Although I have no idea where this thought came from, I find it hard to imagine her accepting this rationale. Her turning pale at the time of my questioning her during our dinner together suggests she was taken in by whatever it was my father told her.

I thought I had a grasp of the full story now I had finished the 'final' chapter. Gathering myself together I flew off to London to find someone to write a screenplay. This sounds very proactive for someone who had just uncovered details of such an unhappy family history. I can look back now and see it was the urge to bring the knowledge of the sexual abuse happening in families out into the open that encouraged me forward. I was also in intellectual mode which would surely have urged me on. What I did not appreciate at the time was I had only accepted part of the story, there was still more to acknowledge and more agonising depths for me to descend into.

Something out of the ordinary occurred while I was on the flight to London. In my journal, I wrote a note to my mother, who had been dead for three years. The note pondered on why we had come together as mother and daughter at this time. Moreover, could we truly expose ourselves and in doing so remove the hyperbole surrounding religious institutions? The words spelt out my pain and the difficulties I envisioned in doing what we had agreed to do. Let me categorically say I have no idea where the rather emotional words I used came from at a time when I was only part way through understanding my life.

Much later, as I was coming to the end of my story, and had probably gained greater insight, I have detailed these words and provided a rationale for my emotional outpouring. However, at this stage, there was no way for me to comprehend a note which appeared to be suggesting some sort of agreement and almost seemed to be otherworldly. It was certainly not the usual sort of note a daughter would write to a mother, even a dead mother. Consequently, it remained in my journal for another five years – forgotten.

What made me think of a screenplay as the path to take, is an interesting question. Perhaps it was because I thought a movie could be more subtle than words, particularly those written by an historian. Did I also unconsciously think a movie could hide more than the written word would divulge?

In London, my attempts to coax someone to write a screenplay failed, but there were some most enjoyable times spent catching up with old friends in a city I consider a second home. Most importantly, I met up with a lady who, unbeknown to her, has been very influential in my holding firm on telling my story.

Sometimes people simply turn up in one's life when the moment is right to help us on our journey. Is it that unknown presence at work? The lady I met at the British Museum while in London is an example. We were on a group history tour to learn about the early Romans. As we sat down to have afternoon tea in the museum's café, I began talking to the lady beside me. She had a calm and very mature look about her. On recognising my accent as Australian, she asked me what I was doing in London. I had reached the stage in my journey where I was prepared to talk about my writing. It had taken some time to get there, but if I took a deep breath, I could fumble my way through and mention the words 'sexual abuse'. I explained to my lady, who responded most unexpectedly. I mentioned the difficulties I was having in finding someone to write my story and how no one wanted to talk about sexual abuse. I was astounded when she quietly said this was particularly the case when it was sexual abuse within a family.

My face must have shown how surprised I was to hear her sympathetic words because she then revealed she was a recently retired family court judge. She went on to explain the courts were full of cases of child sexual abuse within families, but these cases were not being reported or talked about. The book written by Bri Lee in 2015, *Eggshell Skull*, is testimony to the way this is occurring in Australia. My lady judge told me it was important to continue with my writing. To this day when I am having difficulty with what I am writing, the thought of her encouragement inspires me onward.

Although scholarly papers recognise child sexual abuse is a major social problem, finding statistics is a complicated matter, particularly in relation to familial sexual abuse. The silence surrounding the issue ensures any figures would be difficult to take seriously. I have dropped my research into the statistics and am simply left with the feeling the numbers if known, would be very, very worrying.

More to Learn

There was another revelation for me to confront on the next stage of my journey. Gabriel Rolon, the psychologist, claims, 'All the things that happen in our lives are tied to the unconscious. This is because it is, more than anything, the matrix of our repetitions.' And yes, this is demonstrated in my life – the unconscious manifested itself in the repetition of abuse. I would like to think Rolon might suggest that because of where I was at in my life I had little choice in the matter.

As I finished writing about my father, a man appeared in my life. He had just lost his partner, and because of my own experience with loss, I thought I might be able to help him. Ben was an interesting man, intellectually we were a good match, and we had many laughs together. As I write these words, I realise he had similar attributes to Jamie, my second husband. It is intriguing (to me) to note that there was virtually no space between the completion of my writing about those Sunday mornings and meeting this man. I did not realise I was on such a big – and fast – learning curve.

We were very comfortable together. It was almost as though we were already familiar with each other, and then sex reared its head. The decision to have sex was a cold and detached deliberation. There was no emotional consideration on either side. He was still grieving his loss, and I, well, I am not sure where I was. Sex had not been part of my life for a very long time. Once a week Ben and I shared a meal, usually at my house, we went to bed, and then he drove home. As I write these details down, I am sounding very matter-of-fact, but this is how it was.

A memory that really stands out is when he said, on the first time we got together to have sex, "What do you want?" How would someone like me respond to this sort of question? I simply ignored it.

For a sexually damaged person like myself, this arrangement placed me right out of my comfort zone. Not that I understood, at the time, how I had been sexually scarred as a young girl. I now accept any casual sexual relationship is simply not for me. However, I had not yet reached this realisation. I had a vague recollection that between my marriages when I was younger and had casual sex, it was a most unsatisfactory experience for me.

There is no need for me to go into the physical aspects of the relationship between Ben and myself because what is important here is the psychological impact on me and how my history dictated how I handled the situation. I felt rather awkward and completely out of my depth.

My dissatisfaction with our sexual pact meant I eventually called it off. I was in London attempting to find someone to write a screenplay for me and remember writing to him saying I hoped it would not end our friendship. I enjoyed his company just not the business-like sex.

When I arrived home, he stayed away from me which I was a little unhappy about – I thought we were still going to be friends. He then asked me round to his home where he told me he had fallen for another lady (he had been on a dating site). My immediate reaction was to emotionally freeze. All I wanted to do was run away back to my own home, to bury my head and forget about him. I did not process my emotions because I did not know how to.

Six weeks later he contacted me and eventually charmed me into meeting up, and we ended up back in bed. Then he returned to her, and then he came back to me. Unconsciously I think he was emotionally abusing me, and unconsciously I allowed him to do so. As a little girl I had learnt love and abuse go together. As an adult, I obviously still accepted this. The idea that there was any love in this arrangement is something I will touch on later. I had also learnt as a little girl that by shutting down and disconnecting I could handle any abuse.

On the fourth occasion of emotionally shutting down in front of Ben, I realised what I was doing and stopped myself. I faced the issue and all the accompanying pain of losing someone I thought I loved. Others will handle abuse differently, but this was my way, and my guess is many others simply 'shut down' in the same fashion. This was how my mother was able to exist within our family, indeed I probably learnt from her how to close down emotionally.

During my decade of writing, there have been a few professional people I have called upon for counselling. I remember talking to one of these counsellors about the on-off relationship with Ben. She was obviously unhappy for me and during our discussion, my father entered the conversation. She looked astounded when I said, "… but he only touched me." It was the touching as a three-year-old I was remembering: the Sunday mornings had disappeared into the depths of my mind. Little did I know how loaded that comment was and what it revealed about me.

It must be said, at the time I thought 'touching' was okay. The only way I can explain away my comment is, in my mind sexual abuse was about horrific and traumatic details. I had no comprehension of the slow drip of psychological damage which happened to me as a young child. My lack of any enduring feeling of victimhood does not negate the emotional damage done to me.

With the realisation of how I had shut down in front of Ben, the counsellor asked me to write out how I now felt about being abused and what effect I thought this had had upon me. I have often simply written out what is in my head – with no thought or due consideration. The following words were written in this fashion and my calling them 'an epilogue' suggests where I thought I was at in my understanding. Little did I know I was still a long way off comprehending and finishing my story. However, this was an unfiltered pouring out of thoughts and something I truly felt to be accurate at the time.

An Epilogue

How did I end up like this? Distraught at a relationship gone wrong when it wasn't even so good. It was not truly loving, nurturing or even beneficial to me. What the experience has given me is an extremely good lesson in knowing myself and how the effects of my childhood have directed the emotional and physical aspects of my life for almost seventy years. The imprint from those years when I was sexually abused has left me now, as a seventy-plus adult, like a child, bewildered and shattered, not understanding how someone can love and yet hurt me.

The only love I remember as a little girl is the love of my father. My mother was somewhere else. Probably in her own sort of hell. This is the only way I can see it for her because she knew of the ongoing abuse conducted almost in front of her. Perhaps I am being unkind to her. I still do not understand how she was able to accept the activities that went on. However, I learnt if I wanted love from my father, I was required to accept what he did to me. That is, touch me in an unacceptable manner. And so, in my adult life, I have experienced only conditional love, both in my marriage to a much-loved husband and in this latest relationship, my first with another man since the death of my husband ten years ago. I have obviously kept myself for this latest experience so I could learn the essential lesson. Love does not need to be conditional.

Abuse comes in different forms. My father sexually abused me but in the case of these others, it was not sexual abuse. My husband verbally abused me: I would sometimes find myself in an argument that suddenly just appeared, I had no idea where it had originated from. It just happened almost out of the blue, unheralded, and unattended by any preamble or warnings.

Of course, I had learnt from an early age how to handle unpleasant situations. As a child, the coping mechanism I developed was to shut down or freeze out any emotional response. I did not know any other way to handle myself. As an adult I simply carried this on, not realising the consequences of emotional inhibition or disengagement. Thus, within my marriage, because I was unable to talk about or face the verbal assaults when they happened, our married life together was marked by these jolts to our relationship.

So, with the latest liaison, when I was emotionally disturbed by his sexual engagement with another woman I simply disconnected. I froze all thoughts and walked away with my head held high and with an icy heart. Let me say, he was quite in his right to go off with other women, but once was enough. If I was unable to accept that sort of behaviour, I should have been out of the relationship immediately. Instead, I disengaged, nursed my hurts and eventually my heart warmed, and I was charmed back into our friendship.

This last time (the fourth) was different – I did not freeze emotionally. I felt all the hurts that had happened over an eighteen-month period, and which at the time I simply locked out. With this last incident, I faced the consequences of emotional pain and the loss of a loved one. I must ask myself, what sort of love was it? It was conditioned on my accepting his sexual involvement with other women. Just as my father's touching me was a condition of his love.

But then, how do we understand love? It is a word like God – much overused to the extent that it has become almost meaningless and certainly means different things to different people. For me, love and abuse went together. Something I have had to unlearn.

In trying to explain the sexual deviance of my father, I suggested he was a solipsist – someone who is deeply self-absorbed. Perhaps this latest companion was of a similar ilk, and I was simply returning as an adult to the experience I went through as a child. Solipsism has been described as self-absorption and an unawareness of the views or needs of others. This certainly fits in with my companion's reality that only his view was the right one. Whether the topic was religion, friendships (of a sexual nature or not), or even how one should live the last part of one's life, always other positions held were wrong and only his view was right. Applying this word to describe my father is slightly different, but he too was completely self-absorbed, as seen in his hits on women across a restaurant floor. I like to think that if my father knew how he was going to affect his beloved little daughter he would have controlled himself. I fear this is only wishful thinking on my part.

Oh, my dearest father, what a legacy you left me. Yet it has always been up to me to overcome this unfortunate handicap. And I must thank my latest male companion for what I have learnt. It has taken so long for me to reach this understanding about myself. Why? The need to disengage whenever I was involved in a personal trauma must have been so deeply ingrained into my being there was no way for me to process my hurts and the damaging emotions. In this latest relationship, I could not see what was so obvious to others.

If I go back to those early days as a child, I must assume that the mechanism I developed for myself and which I became so good at, became an intrinsic part of my life. It was my means of coping as a child, and it became so as an adult. Shut down and disconnect and I could take anything that was thrown at me. Yet my lack of any engagement meant I was unable to overcome the 'love-abuse' conundrum. As a result of the unhealthy relationship between father and daughter, I have sought out other similar, painful relationships. It was all I knew. If I wanted love, abuse in its various forms became part of it. And this I unconsciously accepted.

The realisation of the long-term effect childhood abuse has had upon me has left me thinking about other abused children and how they have or have not coped. Is there any wonder that sexual abuse within families remains secret and hidden when children, like myself, simply lock out the emotional hurt and pain and take themselves somewhere else to forget? There are many stories of child sexual abuse which are so horrendous and difficult to accept I cannot even get my head around them. Some I am unable to read about. Even though the abuse I suffered pales in comparison, what happened to me as a little girl affected me profoundly, indeed, up until now, it has unconsciously ruled my life. There are probably many ways others have tried to overcome the effects of childhood abuse, however, this is how I handled it and I suspect many others could have taken the same route.

Why is it only now that I have finally learnt this lesson about myself? Like my mother, I have been on my own personal journey. It has been a long process which started with my writing the story of Peggy and her extensive spiritual journey. Telling the story of her spiritual journey became my journey of discovery. From day one, unbeknown to me, I have been trying to tap into what I will call my personal core – that deep place where all is love, acceptance and understanding (and which was damaged when

I was a little girl). This is possibly my mother's 'God within' that she tried, in vain, to find within the Christian church.

Although my own journey in trying to discover this place is very different from my mother's, it has been just as tortuous as her search. With all I have discovered over the last couple of years, there is one dominant issue – I am now willing to be seen and heard rather than remain in hiding with the secrets and inhibitions that come from experiencing child sexual abuse. Alongside this is the realisation I am now free to love without accepting abusive conditions.

This 'epilogue' was written three years ago. It was an eye-opener for me at a time when words had been difficult to form around the issue of sexual abuse. What I now realise is this man, Ben, was like my lady judge, someone who turned up to help me on my journey. While it was a painful experience, I am grateful for his appearance in my life, although I must declare there was still more to play out between us.

The realisation about the arguments which dotted my life with Jamie as being verbal abuse is a very sad revelation for me. My stepdaughter remembers the verbal attacks on me, but she too suffered verbal abuse at the hands of a father who had a troubled childhood. I wonder now how I would have handled the situation if I had recognised his behaviour as abuse while he was still alive.

Writing the Screenplay

Writing for film had previously never been one of my considerations. It was quite simply not my area of expertise. I certainly found it is no easier to tell a story by writing a screenplay. Also, I discovered a screenplay could be open to misinterpretation. The story could so easily go wrong. The odd sentence out of place could provide a completely wrong explanation. For instance, one of my early readers of the screenplay thought he picked up my father and his neighbours, who partied during the 1950s, were possibly part of a paedophile ring. A misplaced inference on my part led to this inaccurate assumption. Although some of my readers may disagree with my deduction, the clarity of the images and words which have come up from my unconscious and are part of my story, do not provide evidence of any paedophile ring. I now appreciate that where there may be intricate complexities involved in a story, the written word, as opposed to a screenplay, is crucial to highlighting what could be critical information. Yet, for the next two years, I carried on with the screenplay. Something was pushing me on.

After arriving back from London, I attended university to learn the craft of writing for film. My lecturer was very helpful and encouraged me in my project. He helped me in the first phase of my writing and even wrote the scene of the children listening to the snow goose story.

Once I thought I had completed writing, some brave friends read my screenplay and offered all sorts of helpful advice. Changes were made – many of them – and finally I had to ask professionals to read it. One reviewer told me my script was not cinematic. She also offered the opinion the father character was interesting. This gave me a different insight into my father, and I accepted that alongside all the negativity around him, my father was a very colourful and 'out there' personality. This needed to be detailed. I rewrote the script and sent it off to another professional reviewer. It was now more cinematic but this time, amongst other imperfections, it was too wordy.

Had I wasted two years of my time learning about screenwriting and then attempting a script? Definitely not. Writing the screenplay was deeply significant and important for me, not that I understood this at the time. In the process of writing the screenplay, I began to feel some of the emotions deep inside me. It was a very confronting period on many fronts. The revisiting of my life seemed so much more fraught than when I wrote the last chapter of my mother's story and recalled the bedroom scene. I am sure this was because, during the previous writing of events in my childhood, I was using an historian's approach, one where there is distance, structured argument, and analysis. In screenwriter mode, I had to fine-tune the details of my story and I was forced to visualise the scenes – one by one – to ensure it was comprehensible to others. I had to take myself back into the depths of my mind and in doing so the story became very personalised and vivid. I was compelled to accept, in part, what had happened and in this acceptance, the unconscious was able to come through. Most importantly, I still needed to feel the deep-rooted emotional pain, and writing the screenplay prised open my emotional wounds.

While putting together the screenplay I began to recognise that I was writing about myself. One of the criticisms from the script reviewer was my story seemed to be about the mother rather than the daughter and I should 'fly closer to the sun', although he did recognise the possible pain in doing so. The notion that it was my story only became known to me – or is the word accepted – the more I wrote the screenplay. My own involvement in the story was something I unconsciously struggled with, and the reviewer picked this up. His comment 'to keep the spotlight on Meaghan' (the daughter) was and even still is something I would rather avoid. Of course, I cannot escape. It is my story I am telling, but it is also my mother's.

Gabor Mate has suggested that unbeknown to us there are unknown forces which drive our decisions and behaviours for many years. The desire to bury my family history and any relevance it held for me was still a strong force within me even as I began to write it out. The reality of familial sexual abuse was almost too unbearable for me to accept, just as it was for my mother. Only slowly did any realisation of this occur to me. Even now I struggle to process the way the many layers hidden unconsciously within my body have been exposed. I am sure there are still more of those layers to be revealed.

My friends worried for me as I struggled to write the screenplay. The anguish I felt was difficult to hide from them. The more I wrote, the more I needed the reminder of my lady judge's words – my writing was important.

It was as I wrote the screenplay that I came to see so clearly how we remember only when we are willing and able. It is then that the unconscious comes into the conscious. For instance, my ruminations about my family show a concern to know, yet the fear of knowing held me back. The phrase *oh no, oh no*, which kept repeating in my mind along with the feeling of dread shows my state of mind which continued for nine months.

Once I faced this fear the opportunity to gain insight arrived. When I asked the question: What was going on under the veneer of our family? the answer seemed to arrive from nowhere. The image I saw is not one I could possibly have made up. It just appeared. And writing those words about family sex on a Sunday morning is something I could not possibly have conjured up. They simply presented themselves.

So too, the realisation of being abused a second and third time, by Ben. I could never have envisaged myself repeating the experience. When I did acknowledge this fact I wrote in my journal:

> '... he is a wolf in sheep's clothing, just like my father. Both charming but with a deep fault line. Can't believe it but think I must – Ben was like my father. How could I go there again? To heal. To acknowledge fully what happened and its effect on an individual.'

Then I wrote, almost foreshadowing my present situation:

> '... so I could bring it out honestly and truthfully into society. To write and be able to explain and demonstrate.'

What I also did around this time was to buy a watercolour painting of a fox silently watching – or was it stalking – a bird sitting high above on a branch. Although now laughing, I was not at the time. I bought the painting to remind myself of the circumstances I had put myself in. I am happy to be able to write that it is no longer in my possession.

It took me a long time to get Ben out of my life. I would constantly tell him simply to leave me alone. There were no hysterical outpourings on my part, just a firm determination for him to be gone from my life

– please. Eventually, I thought he had got on with his life as I had mine.

I met another man, Leon, and so began the sort of story you would expect to see on the set of a movie. I went off to London again to continue writing the screenplay, and while there arranged to meet up with Leon. Here was another man I was very much at ease with – urbane and with a similar interest in the decorative arts, we somehow seemed connected. I interspersed my writing with some good times we had together.

There were four weeks I spent in the Cotswolds when all I did was write and walk and meet up with friends on the odd occasion. It was a most enjoyable time in which I seemed to have found some sort of peace with my writing.

Just as I was due to fly back home, I emailed my screenplay back to myself, purely as a security measure. I am quietly chuckling to myself as I write this, but at the time what occurred was far from a laughing matter. What I did not realise was, Ben had hacked into my computer. Why he would do this is something I still struggle to understand. Perhaps he had heard of my new friend and was jealous. Anyway, he obviously read my screenplay and then had, what could be best described as, a rush of blood to the head. The emails from my computer identified that he was up until the early hours of the morning engaging with the information on my laptop. The first thing he tried to do was access the software I was using to write the screenplay. He attempted to obtain my password from the company, Celtx. What he intended to do if he got into the screenplay is beyond me. This was unsuccessful so he made his next move.

Quite some time ago I had given Ben an unmistakeable portrait of a Māori lady painted in charcoal. It was something I saw as a touristy buy from New Zealand and had given it to him so he could use the gold-trimmed frame for a collection of artwork he was putting together. As I was leaving London, I received an email from an art house in Auckland (who I had previously corresponded with), addressed to me, and suggesting that the painting (a copy of which they included in the email) I had contacted them about was of no interest to them. Ben had apparently asked them how much it was worth and whether they would be prepared to put it to auction, and he used my name to do so. It was difficult to get my head around this because I knew the painting was in Ben's hands, so why was I getting the email? The penny must have eventually dropped somewhere over the Pacific, perhaps.

What I believe threw Ben into such disarray was, inadvertently I called one of my characters in the screenplay by the name of his partner, who had died a couple of years previously. I had taken the name from a real estate agent who had just popped up in my emails and I liked the sound of the name. Only later, once I was home, did the significance of using this name occur to me. I can only think that he used my email address to inform me of what he was up to. Or it could have been his roundabout way of telling me he knew about my new friend, Leon. I am not convinced of either argument and still have difficulty understanding why he behaved so irrationally over the painting.

Once home my computer man helped me sort out my emails and passwords. Then I started to worry. What else could Ben have got into on my computer? I rang the local police, told them the story, and asked them if they would mind passing Ben's house on the odd occasion to possibly make him think about what he had done and so quieten him down. The police did more than drive past his house, they called on him. Again, I am having a little laugh. It was such madness on his part. The police did not tell me what transpired with Ben, but I was told if I wanted to take him to court, they would be behind me.

A few days passed and Ben could not help himself, he sent me a text to let me know about the police knocking on his door. This gave me the opportunity to respond by telling him to never contact me again. He could be in trouble if he did.

Eventually, I learnt from the police they considered Ben to be a narcissist. He was now more understandable to me. All those times he would never see my point of view and most importantly his continual need to control me as his friend was really his narcissism in play.

The similarity between my father and Ben is obvious in the self-centredness both displayed. Earlier I used the word solipsism to describe the self-absorption of my father. Either word is an apt description for these two men who were part of my life at such very different periods. Why has it taken me so long to learn?

Once I realised what had sent Ben into such a state, I deleted the name I assumed had upset him. Then I thought, no, he is not going to control me, so with great delight the name went back into the script. I was learning after all.

The more I rewrote the screenplay the greater my sense of understanding my own story. Complexities emerged and evaporated as I wrote them out. One example can be seen in the family bedroom scene. After the first image appeared, other details presented themselves as if out of nowhere. The unconscious! I began to recognise that the woman in the scene turned her back on the activities happening in the bed. This seems to show something of my mother's reaction to the events taking place and confirms there was more than simply innocent fun going on. Even at this moment, the scene is still too sensitive for me to make any attempt to explain further. Perhaps a little more time is needed.

Also, in the screenplay, there is a closer examination of the children as they interact with the man. As the children frolic around the bed the little girl keeps herself between the man and the little boy, as though she is keeping guard over him. This appears to refer to the thoughts that heralded unaided when I was meditating before the bedroom scene appeared. I was trying to keep my little brother away from my father. These details have come and gone from the screenplay. It was only when I felt brave enough to accept them that I was able to leave them in place. In recent weeks this scene and what was happening has become clearer but for the moment these details rest within me. My use of the word frolic is very significant and shows exactly how far I still had to travel before really accepting what transpired on those Sunday mornings.

On a happier note, I have had greater clarity around the issue of my mother's love for her two children. My attempt to explain Peggy's love in an earlier chapter was inherently correct, but not enough was known at the time to explain it adequately. While coming to the end of writing the screenplay I recalled the various possessions Peggy had bought for her new house in Australia. I was sorting through some old belongings in my garage one day when I came across a painting she bought at that time. It was a brightly coloured picture of a woman holding hands with two children. Both the children are smiling and so is the woman. Immediately I made the connection of a mother with her two children and brought the painting into my study where it remains today.

This painting led me to remember another she bought around the same time. This was of a much darker nature. It was a very modern painting by a local artist which seemed to portray a woman in complete disarray. The figure was distorted and painted black. I remember asking my mother why she bought this painting, and her answer was something quite irrelevant, such as it appealed to her. On Peggy's death, I gave the picture away, but it is obvious that unbeknown to my mother she bought a painting which symbolised her unhappy predicament.

A more cheerful recollection is of the two terracotta figures she bought for her garden. I always liked them and placed them in my own garden soon after she died. I did not see any significance in these figures until after I had finished the screenplay. The figures were of a little boy and girl reading to each other. Now, when I am outside, I can look down at these two figures sitting amongst my camellia trees and a twinkle comes into my eyes. Sometimes a little tear is shed. How slowly I came to comprehend my mother's love for her children. My dismissal of the words in her diary telling us how much she loved us seems quite unjust.

Then there is the significance of the snow goose story. This charming tale became central to the screenplay. Well, that is what I thought. One of the latest drafts of the screenplay opened, like these writings, with the group of children listening to the snow goose story. The script reviewer noted that it felt very poignant and set up a poetic tone. Right from the start I had introduced the idea it was possible for a damaged child to be healed just like the snow goose. There was hope. My professional critic was less than charmed by the way I had handled this important concept: he wanted much more of the snow goose throughout the screenplay. It was 'so powerful' he wrote. My inability to construct more of a narrative around what he called 'recovery and survival' was probably because I was still in recovery mode myself. I am grateful for his sharp analysis and if I ever return to the screenplay I will act upon his advice.

What has just occurred to me is, since using the snow goose story as a central theme in the screenplay I have noticed how flying birds have a calming effect upon me.

Once I had completed writing the story about my mother, I went off to Wellington, New Zealand for three months. I had hoped by being away I could think about what my next writing project would be. Any thoughts of writing my own story had disappeared again. In Wellington, I stayed in an apartment on the harbour. Most mornings would find me captivated by seagulls as they swooped down past my apartment terrace. I wrote in my journal at the time:

'They almost overwhelm me in their beauty … I have tears in my eyes from the strength of freedom, I think it is, that they portray to me. Freedom to be who and what they are.'

Four years before I really began to come to grips with my life there was an inner understanding of what birds meant to me. To complete the picture – in the last few years I moved to a house where, unbeknown to me at the time, white cockatoos swoop down over the trees and into the valley below. The screeching of these birds does not disturb me, as it does others. On the contrary, it is like a call for me to come watch their antics. My exploration of what flying birds mean to us suggests they represent peace, change and freedom. They are also an inspiration to us to aim higher and reach our goals despite the obstacles we might face along the way.

In the screenplay, I always had little Meaghan absolutely enchanted with the snow goose flying so high and, most importantly, free. I now understand more completely my delight around flying birds. Moreover, deep within I feel as long as I can remember the snow goose story all will be well in my world.

Inside My Psyche

Hobart in autumn. The trees in historic Salamanca Place are turning rustic orange. Leaves are beginning to fall. This beautiful area is where I have come to rework my writing of the last eighteen months. There was a feeling of great excitement before leaving Tamborine Mountain. It was rather like the emotional high I experienced before my departure to Paris so many years ago. There was something special waiting for me. Little did I know exactly what it was.

Sensibly I made the decision to leave my inadequate screenwriting skills behind and return to the more comfortable form, for me, of writing for a book. There was a moment when I wondered if fiction was the way for me to tell my story. Apart from the knowledge I would be out of my depth again, there was the realisation of my need to be upfront. I saw it as indispensable to say through my writing, here I am, and this happened to me. It is possible to overcome trauma of this type.

The writing of the screenplay was pivotal in developing my understanding and easing myself into what is possibly the more confronting writing of a memoir. I am unable to escape all those personal pronouns. They are a constant reminder. The screenplay also introduced me to my lecturer and the professional reviewer, and it is their correspondence which highlighted many of the important elements in my family history. Without them, I may have sneaked past writing about some of those challenging experiences.

I notice there is a change of approach to my work. The academic ponderings which have allowed me to stand apart, have given way to an attempt to show more of myself. This is a difficult stance for someone who has buried feelings and hidden behind a façade of indifference for so long, but there is enormous support from the place I now call home.

My apartment sits on the edge of the port in Hobart, and it looks out over the boats and, of course, the seagulls flying between the moorings. There are not as many seagulls as there were in Wellington, but they are here reminding me it is possible to change, and it is possible to open up.

It is the years of emotional suppression that have me most worried for myself. I wonder if the emotional damage done to me as a child and the coping mechanism of disconnecting which I have developed, and fortified, over a period of almost seventy-five years can be remedied. It is a lifetime habit, refined and cultivated to enable me to go out and face the world. More than this, my emotional distance allowed me to feel safe in that world.

Thinking about how I am now, I realise for most of my life I have travelled on the surface. I have skimmed over anything that has confronted me emotionally – unbeknown I have been too fearful of what may be exposed. In my personal life, I have never delved too deeply, nor questioned too much – I have simply accepted how things were. I am not talking about the intellectual questions I have always asked, but questions about how to live a life. What really makes you happy? Who and what sort of person would you like to accompany you in your life? What is the most important aspect of a life if it is to be well lived? Living on the surface has kept me safe and in control.

Control of myself and others has always been my way of operating, although I have never connected this with emotional inadequacy. Gabor has posited, 'Where there is a controlling personality is deep anxiety.' Further, he says, 'Those who build walls against intimacy are not self-regulated, just emotionally frozen.' How I recognise myself in these few sentences. I have often light-heartedly commented to friends that my middle name could be 'anxiety'. It is almost impossible to comprehend the trepidation I have passed through to reach this point in writing out my story. Recently, I wrote, 'Was it really my own life I was looking to understand?' Of course, it was, but here I am almost denying it once again. I must own my story and drop any unease around the telling of it. The script reviewer noticed how I had depicted the daughter as disengaged from what was happening. He suggested there were a few more layers needed for her pain to come to the surface. Denial was the only way to cope for my mother and so too for me – for a long time.

The script reviewer wanted the daughter in the screenplay to have a partner or friend to help make sense of everything, but this was not the reality of the situation. I do not see how it could happen. As my lady judge said, secrecy and silence are the modus operandi of those who experience sexual abuse, and this is particularly the case when families are involved. More importantly, how was I to talk about something I could not really put into words? And if I could speak about it, who would I talk to? No one within my close family was prepared to discuss it with me. And what friend would you worry with a story like this? Perhaps this is why it stayed within me for so long.

As mentioned, it was the interviewing my mother which brought little stirrings up from within me. At the time, around 2012, there was a faint recollection about the happenings in our family – I had seen, and buried, the touching scene twenty years previously – but words around it seemed to elude me. Cathy Caruth, the trauma expert, has suggested the mark of a traumatic experience is that it escapes language. This is what I went through for almost a decade – an unnatural silence. Although words which arise from my unconscious mind are very definite and precise, I have noticed those from my thinking mind are more hesitant and less eloquent: there is almost a slipperiness to these words. And this was where I was in the early days of talking to and writing about my mother and her spiritual journey in my mind.

Once the thought of creating a screenplay entered my head in early 2017, I realised my story had to come out into the open. Gathering myself together I eventually began to quietly tell friends I was sexually abused by my father and left it at that. Even now the bedroom scene is never mentioned. Only those few friends who have read the script know this detail. And interestingly the scene has never been discussed with any of these friends, with one special exception. A very close family friend tentatively asked me about penetration. My negative response gave her visible relief. For me, too, there was comfort in being able to face this topic and answer so easily in the negative.

I had forgotten this issue had already been considered with my lecturer. I have just recalled our email communications when he began to help me with the screenplay. He asked me lots of questions, some of which were very tough, and I answered them with the equally hard truth. However, he too avoided mention of the bedroom scene. Realising his reticence, my email back to him expanded on the scene. I also tried to explain what sort of man I understood my father to be. I wrote:

> 'He was an immoral and weak individual and not strong enough to be really evil. He was degenerate and perverted and only interested in his own sexual needs which I think were possibly of a rather weak nature although obviously he was deeply lecherous.'

I continued with a possible explanation of what he got out of his debauchery:

> 'Perhaps the biggest thrill for this type of man is in his predatory behaviour, as seen in the case of Alex's (the father in the screenplay) dirty talk on the phone to a teenage neighbour. But also, perhaps there is a thrill he gets when he dares to touch his little daughter or later her friends ... whether a thrill equates to an erection or not is beyond me.'

My cool, no-nonsense explanation belied the emotional turmoil that was lurking in my mind unacknowledged. The effect of rereading this email took me by surprise. Tears bubbled up and I had to walk away from my desk. I was still in Tamborine Mountain at the time and the garden became my sanctuary for a few hours. My notes in response to this reaction, identify my distress.

> 'I am so disappointed: obviously, there is still 'stuff' I need to work through. I am still affected by what happened. I am not through it yet. When, oh when?'

There was so much more lingering undetected within my body.

Now, as I engage in rewriting my story in Hobart, the bedroom scene has re-emerged, and I am still deeply troubled by it. I wrote in my journal in recent days:

> 'As I am revisiting the image of us being in that double bed all those years ago, I have developed a very bad case of a migraine in my left eye. I have never had it so bad. This is telling me

something – I'm not seeing something for what it is. I need to break from writing for some reason. I am still not recovered – I think I am looking dispassionately at the situation, but I am still full of emotion over it.'

I stopped writing and went out for some retail therapy. Once back from the shops, I wrote a note to myself about the need to expand on or attempt to explain, those words written down when the picture of the bedroom scene appeared before me. I struggle to accept the words, which referred to family sex on a Sunday morning, and wonder what made me write them. If I am to acknowledge the accuracy of the way the images and words have appeared to help me, I must accept what came to me as authentic – they tell it as it was.

Yesterday, as I was ruminating over confronting the horror of these words, I went for an evening walk to clear my head and came back to my journal. I wrote:

'I want to argue the bedroom scene happened so easily, almost without intent, but I know this is not the case. It would be wrong because I saw the touching scene before the bedroom scene.'

My story has evolved almost as though it has its own pattern of propulsion, forcing me to see things I would rather avoid. If the scene of my father touching me had not appeared or had arrived after the bedroom scene, I could have mounted one of my academic arguments to exonerate him from the Sunday morning activities. This was not the case, of course. I must face the fact my father deliberately and surely knew what he was doing. I cannot argue any other way.

Yesterday's journaling carried on with the emotional honesty which accompanies deep-rooted revelations.

'I want to be an apologist for my father – but I cannot be. I must accept his vile intent. I am so sad at this realisation. What am I to do? … Write it out as it really was. You know deep inside – you know.'

The fragmentation within my consciousness was about to be integrated.

For virtually five years I have read those words about family sex on a Sunday morning, looked at them, and in my mind simply skimmed over them. Knowing but not knowing. It was almost as though I was paying lip service to the idea of being sexually abused. It sat on the surface, not really acknowledged, and certainly not truly felt or accepted. So too, I have been saying the words, 'my father sexually abused me' out loud to others thinking I am strong and brave. The reality is I have not acknowledged them to be true.

It took me a few days to face the fact of my father's deliberate intent to sexually violate me and when I finally accepted it, I took myself back into town, just to walk somewhere and get away from my words. My body was very unhappy with what I had at long last consciously recognised.

As I walked back down Murray Street towards the port and my apartment, my legs appeared to be giving up on me, they did not seem to want to carry me any longer. I was sweaty and my legs felt very weak, I thought I would never make it back. As I rested on one of the many outdoor benches conveniently positioned throughout Hobart, I thought, *I can get myself to Darci & Darci and buy some soup – that could help revive me.* Soup bought, I slowly made my way down to another bench, where I had the soup and felt a little better.

Once back at the apartment, I slept for two hours. My notes at the time reveal my devastation. The following day I wrote:

'I look at my face – it is quite white and drawn at the full realisation – what will be next?'

On reflection, I think my body went into shock at what I was finally forced to acknowledge about my father. Or perhaps it was a release of something held deep within.

With the unlocking of this long-held reality about my family life, other memories have begun to appear. In the early stages of writing my story, I called my childhood memories a wasteland. In Paris eight years ago, all I could recall was listening to the snow goose story as a child. Now, in Hobart, memories are beginning to come to the surface, almost uncalled for. The more I have thought about my life, the more memories have risen from some unknown place to clarify issues I may still be pondering. Perhaps it is because I have become more aware, or more alert to the benefits of memories, rather than the misery of remembering. The big horror that had held me in its grip for so long was now released, and most importantly, accepted. I was free to remember. Now the recall of bits of my life and snippets of long-ago conversations, provide meaning to how my life has been lived.

Both my lecturer and the script reviewer wanted to know how I felt about my parents. I have avoided this issue for a long time, probably because it is difficult for me to find the words to explain in a satisfactory manner. Although, I now realise, before I wrote the screenplay I did answer these questions when my lecturer put them to me. About my father, I wrote:

'He was the only person I felt love from. I remember this feeling from when I was a very little girl – before the age of three, I think. Probably before he touched me … now I feel nothing towards him which is a little sad but probably healthy in the circumstance.'

This was written two years ago and the vacuum surrounding my father and my feelings for him are still with me today.

It is a slightly different situation regarding my mother. I feel great sadness for her – her inability to overcome what happened in our family must have dictated how she lived her life. When my lecturer asked me what I thought my mother got out of her religious journey and whether she ever told anyone, I wrote:

'…it was a journey into oblivion or an attempt, I believe … There is something that makes me think she didn't confess to anyone except perhaps to her mother. My mother's exceptional grief on Nana's death and then her turn to the Christian religion suggests this possibility. Further, that sad look at the end of her life suggests she had not been able to unburden herself.'

In the screenplay, I tried to explain why mothers allow sexual abuse to happen but in my research on the issue, I could not find any straightforward answer. It could be because of deep shame, guilt, or fear but it could possibly be all three.

Further recent research I carried out identified more detailed factors, some of which could help to explain why my mother turned away. The notion that the mentally ill or those with a drug or alcohol problem are more prone to allowing abuse does not apply to my mother. Another category for mothers who look away is the desire to avoid sexual relations with the abuser – this does not sound like my mother either.

There are two factors that almost make sense in the case of Peggy, the most prominent being that she was economically dependent on my father and could not see any way out of her situation. Her father had suffered bankruptcy during the great depression of the 1930s, so as an early teenager she would have felt the effects of poverty and perhaps it was too much for her to consider returning there as a single mother with two children. Her recall, in her journal, of the exact amounts of cash my parents were earning after the war suggests the importance of money to her. That she could be more concerned for financial security than the welfare of her children seems to go hand in hand with her self-centred attitude. I have just turned to my journal and see I wrote only a few months ago:

> 'Was it really about the money, Mum? You left us unprotected so that your own life could be more comfortable. Dad was the big provider and so you went along with it.'

The second factor was that she herself could have been subjected to sexual abuse as a child. Initially, this possibility did not resonate with me. It was her financial consideration over and above anything else that, sadly, rang bells for me.

In recent weeks I have had a rethink about my mother's ability to turn away from the sexual abuse happening before her eyes. Well, it is more an awakening from deep inside – an understanding which just arrived unannounced and that I wrote out at the time.

> 'Dear Peggy, why did you let it happen – why, why, why? Was it because you had been touched by your father too? That is the only reason that appears to me. You were familiar with the experience

and were left frozen as you watched. I wonder if that is what happened, dear Mum? That is the only conjecture I can draw.'

While it was only the touching scene I was recalling here, I now believe she was subjected to sexual abuse as a child. The combination of these two considerations – money and her past experience – would have had a powerful influence on Peggy, although this does not in any way provide her with an excuse for allowing the abuse to happen on her watch.

Living the religious life was so much easier for my mother than facing up to reality. One quite sad moment reveals a lot about Peggy. She was in hospital recovering from a bad fall. I used to breeze into the ward and talk with the other patients. They called us the *Tom and Jerry Show* because of how they saw us reacting together. While I tried to boss her around, she would try to fend me off or just ignore me completely.

One day I was telling one of them about my mother's life, which was so different from other women, and how I was writing about her spiritual journey. Much to the consternation of those who heard her, Peggy piped up with the comment, "Could have done without you." There was a stunned silence in the ward. My mother must have picked up on the atmosphere because her next words were, "I feel for my life to be fulfilled I should have been in a monastery."

I remember soothing the situation by saying out loud to the other patients that I was used to comments like this. Yet, I think my mother firmly believed this about herself. Perhaps an escape to a monastery was a dream which kept her on an even keel. Certainly, life in a monastery would have made it easier for her to attain the silent mind she often talked about. When I was interviewing her, she explained how she saw her silent mind. She said, "I have grown into the deep mind – the silent mind. I look at the trees blowing in the wind but don't think about where the wind is coming from. I don't think about anything." Of course, this is very telling. The ability to not think about anything would have helped her bury any guilt or grief over the happenings in our family.

However, Peggy and I became firm friends in our later years together. Indeed, I could often be heard saying she was more a friend than a mother to me. One of my reflections about our relationship describes her as 'my best friend, yet the affection best friends show each other was missing from our day-to-day life'. We were both tight around emotion and rarely discussed personal details. What was our problem? Were we restrained by our history? We did not think anything of our apparent coolness. This was simply the way it was. The show of any sort of affection was something we did not do. We rarely kissed each other. Towards the end of her life, I began to hug her – she seemed more fragile as she aged. Perhaps emotional restraint was a family thing. Peggy's mother was not demonstrative and always appeared so contained. I do not remember receiving a hug or kiss from Nana either. If there was any show of affection in our family it always came from my father.

A memory has just peeped through of the last meal Peggy and I shared at my home. We had lost electricity throughout our area on Tamborine Mountain, and after four days alone in her own house, her neighbours considered it was time for her to come and stay with me. I had an electricity generator of sorts and the evening she arrived at my house it was working. I cooked a very simple meal of stir fry chicken with vegetables, and we sat at the table together thoroughly enjoying ourselves. She commented, "I never have anything like this to eat at night." This was so special for her. Then we sat and watched a little television which she would not have done for the previous four nights. There were no arguments, no big discussions, it was such a simple and enjoyable time together. Unfortunately, later in the night, unfamiliar with my house and in the dark, she fell down some stairs and had to be taken to hospital. This was the beginning of her slow decline over the following year. It is good to have remembered this, our last night together. It may have been a small moment of connection, but it was very meaningful, I believe, for both of us. It reminded us of the friendship we developed in the last decade of her life.

My thoughts about my father are not so positive. When I first brought the bedroom scene into my consciousness I had wondered if something had been going wrong in our family life for my father to have engaged in sexual abuse. I have just remembered my little brother was not an easy baby. He possibly had colic – I know he cried a lot. This would have made life difficult for my parents, or there might have already been something out of order, something my little brother sensed, and which made him cry. Whatever the difficulties my parents were experiencing, there is no excuse for my father's behaviour. I have accepted now the probable answer to what was happening in our family is my father simply returned to the dissolute ways he was brought up in as a child. Possibly the few years he spent in the army had hardened him, and he reverted to a place where there were no boundaries, no understanding of right from wrong, and where no moral compass existed.

Before I left for Hobart I was thrown into confusion and even chaos when a professional reader I had sent my story to suggested my father was a paedophile. More than this she wanted to know if he had spent time in jail. My lecturer had raised the subject of paedophilia earlier when I was writing the screenplay. This time it was words from my memoir that had seemingly been misunderstood. It was not only screenplays which could be misconstrued, I thought. The second time around I had written and understood much more.

Now, feeling overwhelmed and uncertain, I took myself off to a psychologist. While my sessions with the psychologist have not yet touched on this subject, my understanding of my father and his sexual depravity is that he was rather like a small-time crook, he was not into the big time of sexual perversion such as being involved in a paedophile ring. Put simply, he was a small-time pervert – that is if it is possible to have such a definition. Where he is positioned on the spectrum of sexual abusers I will leave for others to speculate upon.

Around the time of my meltdown, I spoke to my one cousin who is still alive and knew our family well. He is older than me and is one of the cousins we went away with as children for our annual holiday at the beach. I told him I was writing about the sexual abuse I had experienced at the hands of my father. My cousin was not only appalled at hearing about the sexual abuse, he found it very hard to believe. His comment about my father was, "Yes, he was a weak individual but not an evil one." I have not spoken to my cousin since and feel our next conversation will be a difficult one.

One factor about my father needs to be noted. When he died, it was the biggest funeral I had ever attended. Could all those people have got my father wrong? I am conscious of the fact observations from others can only be seen as superficial. And certainly, any cracks within our family were well hidden.

My father was told he should cut back on his drinking otherwise he would have a massive heart attack. And this is what happened. However, there was a story, which I think was started by my husband Jamie, there could have been more to my father's death than a straightforward heart attack. Peggy called the ambulance service to help my father, but he was pronounced dead when they arrived. Jamie always asserted my mother would have held off calling the ambulance until she was sure my father could not be saved. I am smiling at this because it could so easily have been true. There is a comment I hear my mother saying which went something like, "Well I wouldn't have wanted to look after him as a vegetable." This remark is such a reflection of the self-centred individual my mother was, but I cannot definitively confirm she did say those words. I do remember talking her through what happened at the time, and she told me he kept asking her to get the doctor, which she never did. Could it be the doctor would have got there quicker and she knew this? I do believe though that Jamie's conjecture has more to do with his light-hearted imaginings (or were they dark thoughts) than the reality of what happened at the time.

I swing between thinking good of my parents and then the worst of them. I am also aware that it is a common trait in those who have been abused to play down what has happened to them. My understanding and acceptance of how relevant the unconscious is in bringing memories into my conscious mind will help me reveal other unpleasant scenes from my life if that is necessary. For the moment my recall is only as I have detailed it so far. I have questioned myself as to whether there could be more disagreeable elements to my story which remain hidden. During the past year, I faced this possible nightmare by utilising my tapping exercise and asking if there was anything else I needed to know. With great relief, a big cross (as in the negative) appeared as an image.

There have been several times I have been told I should be very angry with my parents. I have wondered where that anger has gone and have tried to bring it out into the open through writing in my journal. It is such a half-hearted attempt at anger the words are almost inappropriate. The problem is, I do not feel any great anger. My hesitancy in venting anger is reflected in the beginning of one note to my father. I start with 'My dear father'. Then the academic in me comes out and all I want to know is why. In another note, I try to explain what he took from me with his behaviour.

'Your love was tainted and not true and it has taken a long time for me to accept this within myself. You destroyed the joy I had to be on this earth – that happy, happy child became anxious and confused.'

The end of this note declares, 'Shame on you for even contemplating it.' There are three full pages of notes written in my journal to a father I was desperately trying to understand. The most significant issue coming up in these pages is the question: How could you do this to the child you professed to love so much?

Part of what I wrote down while trying to summon up rage against my mother is equally feeble. I wrote:

'Should I be angry with my mother for not protecting me? Was she weak? My pity and sadness for her – is this misplaced? Why do I not feel very, very angry with both my parents? Am I being too understanding? Or not understanding at all?'

My pondering led me to wonder about the strong and courageous woman who left her country at the age of eighty-four to live in another. What happened to this robust woman when she was young? How could she turn her back on her children? My musing eventually saw me write, 'Oh, oh, dear Peggy – is there something else to this that I haven't realised yet?' And yes, there was something else, although, at the time of writing this note I was still a few weeks from any comprehension. Then I wrote down what is a continuing worry for me: 'Is it that I am emotionally frozen about this subject – still?'

Recently, it was with great relief that I listened to my psychologist's explanation of what is called, in her field, the 'Unforgiveness Hook'.

The idea is, that if as in my case, the abusers and the abused stay hooked together in unforgiveness, it will never be possible to live out a happy and rewarding life. For me, she explained, I would have to let my mother and father off the hook – that is, forgive them – before I can get off the hook myself.

Somehow, I did let my parents off the hook. I cannot explain how or when this happened, but my lack of anger is evident in the way I am unable to write out any truly angry words when I think of them.

My opening up to my lecturer and the rereading of those early emails I sent to him revealed a few issues I quite conveniently forgot about. Something that was important to him was, 'How YOU felt then and NOW about things?' This was a central matter for the reviewer as well. I am not sure I can answer my lecturer's question even now. I do not know how I really felt then (as a child). How I feel at this moment could change by the time I complete my writing. I sometimes think the story I have written lacks any proper order because of its ever-changing nature. The more that is unravelled the more changes appear. The script reviewer commented, the daughter 'feels like a lost soul looking for answers … even after the final scenes, there is a sense she is not healed or able to move on with her life.' My writing now is part of the healing process – this is my big hope.

I have been told (not by professionals) to simply move on, to leave my past in the past and enjoy life as it is today. Someone, a few months ago, who was worried for my mental health, told me to "Just get over it, Kay." The lack of empathy in this comment was disturbing to me at the time, to the extent I picked up my handbag and walked out of the house. This friend obviously had no understanding of the emotional consequences inherent in cases of sexual abuse. It must be said, again, there are times I wish I could just drop the telling of my story, yet I feel there is something deep inside driving me on.

On a lighter note, a glimpse into my mindset can be seen in my reaction to hearing tales of positive, caring childhoods. I almost feel jealous when I hear comments from people, perhaps who are being interviewed on television or radio, about how wonderful their childhood was and all the positive things they learnt from their parents. Jealousy is usually not one of my negative traits, but I am aware of it when I hear these lovely stories about home life. I have always dreamed about what it would have been like to grow up within a nurturing family. When I was asked by my lecturer what I would change if I could, I told him, "I would have loved to have been brought up in a loving, educated family." The reality of living within a family such as this is almost beyond my imagination. I am unable to envisage how it would play out.

The journey I have been on is long, just as my mother's was, and I am not sure I have reached the end yet. I think I am there and then something else happens. For instance, the words *leave me alone, leave me alone,* have been coming up out of nowhere in the last few months. I have sometimes felt a disquiet, almost depression, and these words come into my mind: they are said quietly in my head, although there is a very definite quality about them. I have no idea what they are referring to. Recently, understanding simply appeared and I wrote in my journal, 'I know where these words come from – deep in my past when I was a little girl. Only now am I prepared to face them.' And yes, I feel I said these words to my father at some time.

On becoming aware of this, I went into a panic, crying out I needed help to process this 'knowing'. Over a few hours, I calmed myself and relaxed into the knowledge. Now I have recognised what this phrase is about, the words have left my head. They rose from my unconscious and will not bother me again.

As I now redraft my original writing in Hobart, I have remembered the other recent, and only other time I said these words. It was this phrase I returned to – quietly and doggedly – in my attempt to be rid of the narcissist, Ben. If I ever needed proof of how my childhood trauma stayed with me, this insight demonstrates it.

Thinking about this phrase has made me look at how the abuse from my father stopped. I do not know for sure when or how it came to an end. I wonder at my courage in saying these words to my father. Perhaps something had occurred to give me extra strength. Did my mother help bring the abuse to an end? I have blanked out whatever happened and am happy to continue to do so. There is no need to know everything. My wanting to go to church to give thanks, around the age of eight, suggests the abuse had ended by then. That it was my father, and not my mother, who was prepared to take me to church is thought-provoking – certainly for me. Perhaps this is another example of my father's role as caregiver in our family.

My story is about the slow revelation, or awareness, that comes up from the unconscious when an individual is ready. I did not convince the script reviewer of this. His comment, 'For the plot to work, we need the enormity of the abuse to slowly unravel.' This was a vital element in my thinking – to tell the uncompromising truth of my early childhood as it slowly became untangled from inside me. My inadequacies around script writing meant I did not manage to get this across, but now that I am using memoir, I have more chance of showing this slow unravelling.

Sometimes I have wondered, did this happen to me – really? Then I think about how I am or have been for most of my lifetime; emotionally closed, anxious, and controlling. These few words are an adequate summation of how I have handled myself in the outside world. So I tell myself something must have happened for me to go through life in this way. Then I believe in myself and my story again.

The script reviewer had plenty of questions which I thought I had answered. How had the abuse impacted Meaghan as an adult? Does she have trust issues? What choices had she made in her life that she would not have chosen without the abuse in her past? I realise now that some of these questions were answered with explanations or words in the script, but it is the adage, 'show, don't tell' that is important in film. I now understand where I went wrong in the writing of my screenplay.

Some of the choices I have made in my life help to tell my story. Most importantly there was the decision not to have children. It has just occurred to me, my refusal to play with dolls as a young girl was an early indicator of my future decision – and of my history. Dolls, and the activities which are part of playing with them, simply did not appeal to me. I can only imagine what sort of behaviour is involved in playing with dolls. I do remember playing with puppets on strings, though. Heavens, I was into control so early.

Marriage was another area I did not want to venture into. The fact I was married twice to much older men speaks for itself. My parents, of course, were not good role models, although my brother's chief desire as a young lad was to marry and have children. This gives me hope that he was not abused as a small boy.

Then there is my inclination to enjoy the company of men who are players – just like my father. Not that I am suggesting they touched children. I have a small list of men who have been significant in my life and all of them were or are players – someone who can have more than one sexual affair happening at the same time. Even Steve, from my youth, eventually became a player. The only important man in my life who is not on the list is my first husband, Bill. He did not fit into the mould my father had set up for me, where love, sex, and betrayal intertwined.

In the notes to my father, when I was trying to be angry with him, I explained how he had affected my relationships with men:

'You set me up for a lifetime of anguish – never feeling safe, always anxious, and mostly choosing the wrong sort of man – most of them were like you ... my anxiety around sex left me confused and not understanding – of course – because you had interfered with my normal growing up around the subject.'

There are parts of this note which became quite strident as I compared my father with these players, who I must emphasise were very much welcomed into my life, including for many years my second husband, Jamie. Freud's notion that the unconscious mind is the primary source of human behaviour is clearly behind my choice of these male companions. The realisation of my partiality for men who are players is only a recent awareness, and my hope is this knowledge will help me avoid this type of man again.

As already mentioned, a significant impact abuse has had on me is the emotional avoidance I have practised from my earliest days. I have often been designated a very private person. This can easily be seen as shorthand for someone who does not give much away in personal terms, keeps very much to themselves, and remains in control. An exchange with a close friend illustrates this attitude. She was telling me about some gossipy story related to me when she looked at me closely and said, "You don't care, do you?" Really, I did very much care, but my ability to remain emotionally detached hid my true feelings.

Another example of my need to be in control can be seen in the fact I have often declared I have never fallen in love. Of course, I could never allow myself to lose control, moreover, this was something I was quite proud of. Although I consider that I have loved, I see this as different to falling in love. I realise now that this indulgence is something I have never allowed myself. The use of the word indulgence says it all. Obviously, I still find it hard to imagine losing myself to love. I must admit I am sceptical about the idea of love. It is probable I do not trust the word, or the feeling love is meant to invoke. It is self-evident this has a lot to do with my relationship with my father.

The development of Attachment Theory in psychology has been an important tool for understanding the way children acquire normal social and emotional development. John Bowlby's original theory posited that it was during the first six months of a child's life that a relationship with at least one primary caregiver was required for normal development. Looking at myself, if the feeling of being loved by my father as a young child is true, my emotional development should be normal. However, it is not. Again, I ask myself, how reliable is my memory of being loved by my father in those early years of my life? It was a feeling I carried with me for a good chunk of my life, and I consider it to be a genuine part of me.

Words from my mother's journal reveal my very early contentment. She writes, 'There was so much joy in caring for this beautiful, alert and happy baby.'

My psychologist has explained how this feeling of being secure in my father's love was disrupted by the dual message I received. The message of love was disturbed by the worry my little girl self felt when in the double bed on Sunday mornings: What was Daddy doing? Although I was too young to have known the right or wrong of what was occurring, the worry I felt was identified during a recent session with my psychologist.

The idea I felt a great love from my father in my first years continues to worry away at me. Did I make this up to help myself through my trauma as a little girl? Or even as an adult, have I exaggerated this feeling so that I could feel okay about myself – I was lovable? I have had to face this concern because it is one of the important issues to my story and so, with great reluctance, today I returned to my knee-tapping exercise. I asked the question: Was the love I felt from my father as a little girl authentic – was it true? With great relief, an image appeared of my father holding me, as a very little girl, in his arms and he is looking down at me and smiling. This is like the photograph at home – the one which gives me a warm glow whenever I look at it. There is such relief with this realisation, tears are forming.

Something I have accepted about myself recently is when I am having an emotional meltdown my body lets me know. Sometimes I am given a warning when I am about to reach deep inside myself, such as in the example of my heart problem in Auckland, and my eye migraine here in Hobart. Other times, such as when I am having emotional issues with men, my body informs me. When I was engaged in the on-off relationship with Ben, my narcissist friend, a lip sore would appear – usually in the same spot – and always when I realised what he was up to with the other woman. The lip sore developed four times, a week or so after the recognition that once again I had got it wrong.

I must also confess to the fact that it was only with the appearance of the lip sore that I recognised my emotional state. Research has shown the inhibiting effect of chronic stress on the immune system. Gabor has posited, that those of us who are exposed to stressors we cannot escape either because they are not recognised or because there is no control over them, can suffer permanent damage to the body. I now understand why the sugar levels in my blood border on being too high despite my healthy lifestyle. The adrenaline utilised in my states of anxiety is pushing my blood sugar higher than it should be.

Recently, I read that sexual trauma symptoms can manifest physically, such as in the experience of reoccurring gynaecological, gastrointestinal, and cardiovascular problems. While concerns about my fluttering heart are relatively recent and are usually related to some issue I may be feeling about a man in my life, I have struggled with gynaecological and digestive problems throughout my life. Hopefully, these concerns will begin to lessen.

How do I feel now all this is out in the open? I would not be me if I was not anxious. I constantly ask myself: Why trawl through my life in this way? Could it be more productive to leave it all alone and get on with living in the moment? Then I realise I need to make sure I have broken the behaviour of a lifetime. I need to understand how my emotional immaturity was set up by my early childhood experiences. Only then will I be able to thrive. Moreover, and perhaps more importantly, there is my offering to the world – an explanation of how sexual abuse in families can happen and how it is possible to recover and even flourish.

There is a phrase that comes into my mind that gives me much hope for myself. It is like the phrase 'leave me alone'. The phrase 'darling heart' comes up from somewhere unknown to me, although it arrives only occasionally and often when I am walking along our country lanes. I have no idea what these words are about – whose heart does this phrase refer to anyway? Mine perhaps, but why? Yesterday I tried to remember these words with my conscious mind and could not. I wrote in my journal:

'How amazing! Have been trying to remember the few words about a heart which come into my mind. My conscious mind cannot bring those words up. They are forgotten for this moment. These words are not learnt, they are from the unconscious. Eventually they will arise again – gently and very definitely. I have no idea whose heart is in the frame – mine, a dear friend or even a loved one departed from this world. Perhaps it is that Unknown Presence that accompanies us on our journey through life. I wait to recall again.'

Six hours later I wrote:

'For the last few hours the words have been coming into my mind – quite graciously and all loving – the words are 'darling heart'. I have no idea who or what these words refer to, but there is something my unconscious wants me to know.'

One of my dear friends has recently reminded me of the acronym HELP, which is formed by the initial letters of 'Hello Eternal Loving Presence'. This is probably my mother's 'kingdom of God within' which she searched for when she first left the Christian church. My own experience with this presence occurred when I had breast cancer many years ago. Jamie and I were in the Blue Mountains for a long weekend. We had gone there to relax, enjoy some good food and take in the clear mountain air. One early evening I was alone in the hotel lounge and in a deep meditation when a bright light in a star-like formation appeared high up and off to the left. One of the points of the star was aimed directly at my right breast where the cancer had been. I understood then I would recover from cancer.

A few days ago, I decided to find out exactly what, or who, the darling heart phrase was about. My knee-tapping exercise came out of the closet. I rarely use this exercise, because I think that if I was to overuse or misuse it there could be the possibility of my losing this valuable tool. I started to meditate and to tap my knees and asked the question: What is the phrase darling heart about? And of course, the picture that formed was of a bright light off to the left and high up beaming down at me. There were no star-like points this time, just a warm glow from the light. I had an idea about that unknown presence, but it was now confirmed. I have taken this picture from my unconscious to mean I am supported no matter where I am and at what stage I am at on my journey.

Strange Thoughts from Hobart

It is early evening and Hobart is beginning to light up. My late afternoon walks have been very beneficial in helping me release the emotion built up from my writing. Often, I take myself up to and through historic Battery Point, named after a battery of guns which were established there as part of Hobart's coastal defences in 1818. It is recognised as the best-preserved colonial-era suburb in Australia. It is also here the gardens remind me of England, with all the exotic plants we find so difficult to grow in Queensland. The buttercup yellow of the blossoms on the mahonia has caught my eye. The yellow seems so much more alive in this cool climate. My attempts to grow mahonia on Tamborine Mountain are obviously a dismal failure: it looks to be a completely different plant here. Relaxing and invigorating at the same time, these strolls through this elegant area provide me with a final letting go for the day.

As I come to the end of telling my story, I think about the insights which still appear to me unannounced and seem to tear me apart as some new aspect of my life is revealed. The most important understanding, so far, is the one where I have made the connection between having sex and the idea of being loved. The deep love I felt from my father before I turned three, can be seen in any of the photographs from the period.

We were such a relaxed and happy little family. What I recognise now is the one person who I remember loving me also introduced sex into our relationship. I am now able to grasp that at the time I engaged in sex with my narcissist friend, Ben, I had confused the act of having sex with being loved. I was emotionally still very much that child, in sexual terms, when I met my former friend.

Yet the connection between sex and love played out within my next relationship. I thought there was love involved with my London friend, Leon. Well, there was sex – it has taken a long time to recognise my mistake. At least this time, when I learnt he had another woman friend I was out of the relationship. This was not an easy thing for me to do and I continue to tell myself I should be encouraged by the emotional distress which still clings to me. At least I am now allowing myself to feel.

As I have arrived at certain stages in the journey to uncover my internal scars and I think I have reached, or almost reached, the end – I become aware of new information and new feelings. For instance, after writing the screenplay I thought I was like a technician simply bringing all the pieces of my story together. All emotion was expended. How premature was this thought? There was still Hobart for me to experience. I am glad my friends are not here to see me having to face the various jolts to my psyche as I process new information.

The most difficult, so far, has been the conscious understanding of my father's focused intention to sexually abuse me. The acceptance of this truth has left me feeling as though there is a dull ache throughout my body. Accepting but not wanting to – still. How could he if he truly loved me? I cannot use my rational mind to explain or overcome this ache for the moment. Throughout the last decade, and since Jamie's death, an ache has often accompanied me. I have pondered on the way it arises and then disappears. My last contemplation on this ache was only a few days ago. During the intermission of a classical concert when I was probably in quite a relaxed state I wrote:

> 'What is this ache? A soul thing? Why would a soul ache? For something it needs. Nourishment, love – I think that is what the ache is about. A need to be loved.'

I accept this love will come at the right time when I am ready.

Over the last ten days, I have noticed when I stop to talk with someone, and they ask me what I am writing about, I do not tell them. My upfront self seems to have disappeared and I become rather wishy-washy and say something like, "I'm writing a family history." Previously I would always use the words sexually abused, almost as an act of defiance. Now, as the truth of what happened to me has become a reality, it is not so easy for me to say those words. It is not because I want to deny the fact, I think I am still processing this most unpalatable truth.

A help-mate arrived this morning in the form of my breakfast companion. Most mornings I walk through the dock area and into tree-lined Salamanca Square, pick up a newspaper and have breakfast of coffee and toast at Darci & Darci. This morning sitting beside me was a woman, rather like my lady judge, who had a kind and knowing face. When she asked me what I was writing about, I gave her the now usual oblique reply, but this time I must have had a look on my face which gave me away. Her response has lightened my mood. She remarked, "We are all human, and very similar. If you look at any family, you will find unpleasant factors involved in the make-up of the whole." I will not forget her words.

My eye is beginning to play up again – there must be something I am refusing to see. My body is feeling weak, too. This was a recognition of my condition a few days ago, but I am now feeling stronger and will tackle an issue I have had trouble accepting and which is probably the source of my eye migraine.

As a person of the mind, the notion that we make pre-birth contracts is rather too out there for me. Yet, I want to suggest I made a 'soul contract' with my mother. I know – this is almost a step too far. Still, I cannot ignore those words I have previously mentioned, and which have sat in my journal unheeded. It was on the flight to London, where I had hoped to talk with someone about writing a screenplay when I wrote that note to my long-dead mother expressing my doubts about what seemed to be some sort of agreement we had made.

'Can we do it, Mama? Can we really expose ourselves to the world? This is what we came here for – why? What for? I think to help others. To remove the hyperbole, the nonsense of religious institutions. Help me say it as it is. Can I do it? Yes, yes – I will. Why such pain? Is it from all those years ago – built up?'

These words simply did not make any sense to me when I wrote them down five years ago. The idea of a contract – that is, a soul contract – provides meaning to these hesitant and almost senseless phrases. There were also the words I wrote out while trying to be angry with my mother a few months back; when I wondered if there was something more I needed to comprehend about our story. Was it the contract I still needed to confront?

The notion of making a contract of this type sits rather awkwardly with me. Although in the past I bought Caroline Myss's book *Sacred Contracts* which explores the way a sacred contract can shine a light on the purpose and meaning of one's life, I was unable to engage with her thoughts on the subject and gave the book away. So too, many years previously, I remember reading a book written by an American doctor who had hypnotised a group of his patients and asked them to go back to the time just before they were born, when they made their 'soul contract'. One amusing story from the book was about a man, who on learning he would have to go back and reconnect with his mother remarked, "Oh, not her again." This droll comment is all I can recall from the book. Obviously, at the time I had an interest in this subject, but not enough for me to hold onto the details in any significant way.

With my new-found perception, there are several inferences I can take from the words I wrote to my mother. Firstly, there is the hint of a contract which I can only see as coming from my unconscious. This was not a discussion I ever had with Peggy, and it is something I have never thought about with reference to myself. More than this, it is an issue I had previously not given any thought to. I have mentioned earlier how much easier it would be to not write my story, but something seemed to be driving me on. The contract?

Secondly, the use of the word hyperbole requires an explanation. I have never used it before or since, and at the time of reading the word in my journal I had to check in the dictionary that I understood its meaning. Where did the word come from?

Thirdly, I have wondered why I constantly wanted to write about my mother; again and again, it was her story that rose to the forefront instead of mine. Understanding Peggy and her religious journey was so important to me. Was this because I needed to be able to fully comprehend the path she took? It was so different from my own.

Early in the writing of this story, I sent a draft off for a developmental edit. The editor was extremely helpful, although she wanted the many references to my mother diluted. Comments such as 'too much about Mum' or 'I'm wanting to hear about you, not Mum' were dotted throughout her commentary. At this early stage, the notion of a contract had not appeared in my story. Even so, I was unable to remove Peggy from my story. Although I had no idea why, it seemed the spiritual journey my mother embarked on, was somehow fundamental to my own story. My inability to limit references to Peggy can be seen in relation to the contract we made with each other. She was my partner.

Long ago, in Paris, I had an inkling there was a connection between our two stories when I deliberated in my little red book whether I should tell the two narratives side by side. Even though at the time I did not fully grasp I had a story to tell about myself, I had a hunch about it.

The difference between my mother's journey and my own is quite definite and I believe we made our contract to expose our quite diverse approaches to handling the sexual abuse within our family. While she used religion to cover up, I attempt to uncover. She kept herself outside our trauma as opposed to my attempt to go inside. Unlike me, Peggy, although in denial, could recall the sexual abuse in our family. I have had to bring it up from my unconscious.

Although she travelled down so many religious paths, they were unable to provide her with the comfort and support she searched for. I had to fully appreciate the depth of her engagement with the various religious organisations she belonged to so that I could recognise their shortcomings in helping her to overcome the trauma of the sexual abuse within our family. She was able to escape from her past, even though only temporarily, under the guidance and dictates of religious dogma. Peggy's almost exhausting journey into the religious provides an example of the way religion is unable to help overcome the effects of such evils as sexual abuse in our society. Our contract was made, I believe, to help identify this lack within the various religions.

The difficulties of travelling down my path are evident in the emotional lows I have experienced as I have tried to unpick my life. While my mother ran from one religion to another, I hid until I could not hide any longer. The more I wrote, the more it became impossible to hide from myself and the closer I came to that inner core of knowing. Unconsciously, I knew there was something unpleasant about my life. So, a lifetime of skimming over the surface, not looking too deeply and not asking the necessary questions, kept me safe. Until now.

I have just recalled a brief conversation I had with my mother many years ago. It helps to clarify that she knew what she was getting involved in, regarding my father. At the time I had difficulty understanding why, as a mother, she would tell me of this occasion in her life. Before they married my mother worked in a government office and apparently, my father's name came up in the files she was reviewing. Perhaps she looked up his name deliberately. I cannot recall the exact details except that she saw his name in reference to an incident where he had lied to the authorities about a friend's involvement in an issue which was deemed morally wrong. He had perjured himself for his dissipated friend. This tells me Peggy knew my father lacked moral integrity. Although she told me she was very shocked by what she uncovered, she obviously carried on with the relationship.

My understanding, now, of why she would tell me of this incident is because in some way this is connected to the 'contract' we made with each other. Was it because she had unconsciously found the perfect accomplice to help carry out our contract? The fact I have remembered this conversation seems pertinent to my attempts to articulate something so unfamiliar to me.

While I have trouble accepting the notion of a contract, it helps explain some of the anomalies in my story. There was the deep love I felt for my father as a young child, and which he felt for me, but he could sexually abuse me. Was there something 'other' involved?

It has been put to me that it was a different era when the abuse occurred. A time when children were seen but not heard and a child's perspective was not important; children's humanity was almost not recognised and any consequences from bad behaviour towards them were not acknowledged. Another line of reasoning advocates the idea that because my father loved me so much, he became confused about love and sex. Neither argument is acceptable to me because my father participated in various debauched sexual activities with other women and girls. He was in fact the ideal candidate to participate in our contract – an immoral character. And this I must recognise.

Then there was the coldness of my mother in our earlier years together, changing to a more intimate and warmer friendship towards the end of her life. Apart from her religious tendencies, we had begun to think alike and became joined in a bond of sorts. She wrote in her journal:

> 'In looking back over the last two and half years, Kay, the most important part or aspect of my being here is to have been so much with you and Jamie and to have been part of your life during this time.'

She then made the comment she was happier living in Australia than in New Zealand. This was a big admission for my Kiwi mother.

There is also the deep emotion I felt, but could not understand why, as I slowly became aware of the need to write about Peggy's spiritual journey as less than perfect. Segments in my journal reveal the disturbing phase I went through.

> 'I must write of your spiritual arrogance, my dearest Mama. I am not sure why I need to do this, but I do! Why? Am breaking, am breaking but it is the truth.'

And further on:

> 'I am crying without consolation. Nothing seems to be able to stop my terrible tears. They are tears of desolation.'

These highly disturbing words are interspersed with an intellectual knowing:

> 'It is my own journey of getting over this having to show Peggy up – it is just an exercise but so important. She will not feel hurt or offended – it is what we agreed to do … there is some deep connection I have with Peggy that is so disturbing me – makes me so wretched – so sad. It is my problem to overcome. I know she will be looking down telling me to pull myself together.'

The end note to myself says, 'Get over it, K.'

These were thoughts I simply could not comprehend at the time of writing the narrative about my mother's life in 2015. Yet my persistence is saying something. Perhaps my constant desire to tell her story, although under such painful circumstances, can be understood with reference to the contract. My need to denounce her spiritual journey, almost unwillingly, could be tied to our agreement.

There was another incident which offers further evidence of strange otherworldly events around this time. It was the first Christmas after Peggy's death, and I went to an evening carol service at my mother's old church. I had attended church on previous Christmas occasions, so I did not consider this an unusual thing to be doing. Except this time, for some unknown reason, I was very alert to what was happening in the church and what was being said. Particularly, I took notice of the words in the carols and hymns we were called upon to sing. And I was left bewildered at the sometimes absurd wording. I was almost shocked at sentences which did not seem to make sense.

I became flustered, even rattled, and could not wait to leave the church and hurry home. On arrival, my cat, Benny, greeted me quite strangely. Like me, he seemed agitated about something, to the extent I walked through the house thinking there could have been someone in the house who had disturbed him. Telling him there was no one in the house, I walked into the study where I was writing my mother's story. I looked back at him standing in the hallway, and said, "See, there's no one here," but his eyes were wide open, and he seemed quite terrified in that moment.

At the time I felt this was an 'out of this world' experience but had no way of understanding what was involved. Was Benny seeing the spirit of my dead mother? If so, why had she appeared? Was she signalling to me my disquiet over the words in the carols was an appropriate response? Or perhaps not. At that point in time, I was unable to grasp the implications behind these out-of-the-ordinary happenings. Looking through my journal I see a note written a few days later, 'Benny is now scared of being inside.' He eventually calmed down and this also was noted in my journal. This almost ghostly experience makes sense if placed alongside the notion of our entering into a contract. Benny's curious stance tallies with my equally troubling acknowledgement of the contract.

There is another argument for accepting the idea of a soul contract made between Peggy and myself. Although we never engaged in any personal discussions on a mother-daughter level, Peggy's sharing of information about her intimate relationships with me suggests she was talking with someone she regarded as a collaborator, not simply a daughter. Her telling me of the evidence she uncovered about my father in her work office, her disclosure of her love for an American soldier, and her hints of an affair within her local neighbourhood; was she revealing, although in a rather inexplicable manner, how she came to make the choice of marrying my father?

While some of my deductions about our soul contract could be seen as perplexing, the urge to write this story has been simple and clear-cut. Whether it was the contract with Peggy or something else ethereal and equally difficult to figure out, I cannot ignore the very definite feeling from within that my story needed to be told. This is a knowing not to be disregarded. As I prepare to leave Hobart, my sense is that I will hold firm and complete our contract.

Finally, as I come to the end of writing my history, there are a few words I would like to say to that little girl who was sexually abused by her father. 'Remember you made the contract with Peggy, and you have carried it out. Remember you felt unconditional love from your father, he just was not able to maintain it. While you hanker for this sort of love again, you have felt it and are therefore lucky. And you were so very fortunate because you heard the snow goose story. It gave you hope and the possibility of better days to come. You may have been very confused and unconsciously damaged. You lost all sense of fun and lightness but know it is beginning to come back – now.'

This morning, as I tried to walk hand in hand with my little girl self, tears began to form far too quickly for comfort. I have promised myself each morning as I walk to the café for breakfast, I will take her with me and quietly talk with her until we are gently smiling together.

A week has gone by and this afternoon the walk with my little girl self was a delight. She was about five years old with her light-brown hair plaited in two pigtails. She was wearing a lightly-coloured dress with little embroidered animals dotted all over the front, and there was a bow in the same fabric, tied neatly at the back. She smiled up at me as she skipped along holding my hand. She is so happy.

The heaviness which has usually accompanied me throughout my life is beginning to lift. There is a sense of an enormous weight having been lifted off my shoulders. During the last year, I have had periods of lightness; for example, when I visited what I have left of my family in the South Island of New Zealand. There, I detected a carefree and more frivolous woman wanting to reveal herself. Sometimes, when I am with my close friends on Tamborine Mountain, I feel that sunny and untroubled disposition I was born with, come to the fore.

Final Revelations – at Home

It is that time for the cockatoos. They are shrieking and swooping through the trees into the valley below my house. Tamborine Mountain is part of a large plateau, 525 metres at its highest point, and my property sits on an edge overlooking the Gold Coast. It is surrounded by rainforest. This wooded area is a happy eating place for these large white parrots – berries and seeds are in abundance for them. There has even been a visit to my big bird path in the lower garden from two yellow-tailed black cockatoos. Google tells me these beautiful birds represent a powerful spiritual symbol in Australian Dreaming and are associated with auspicious outcomes including emotional freedom, joy, and contentment. Perhaps my life is about to change. I must add the appearance of these birds is also related to the possibility of rain.

Early evening at my desk and I ponder on almost a decade of writing, and the question of where this memoir will end up has arisen. Will the motivation which has been with me throughout my writing endure? Will I stick it out through the ordeal of publication? Or will it be enough to have finally understood what my life has been about? If I keep in front of my mind the reason for telling this story, I will stay strong and fulfil the contract Peggy and I made.

The question from my lecturer five years ago, 'What is it you want others to take from what happened to you?' holds the key to my perseverance. At the time I had not gone through the struggles of confronting my past and it was easy for me to answer him. I wrote:

'Most importantly, we never know what is going on within families behind closed doors. I think the sexual abuse that occurs in institutions and the workplace can happen more easily because it is so prevalent within families.'

As a further explanation, I added:

'The sexual abuse in my story is not of an horrific sort as in some cases in our society but is of a sneaky, underhand nature where an authoritative figure exploits and violates the responsibilities he has been given. I suspect this is quite pervasive in our culture.'

The conclusion here reads as obvious now, but back then the public airing of various sexual misdemeanours within society had not been fully brought out into the open. Still though, familial sexual abuse remains buried in secrecy. Surrounding the whole subject there is an elusiveness brought on by the echo of what is unvoiced. It is for this reason it needs to be talked about and why I suggested to my lecturer a movie would be a good option because it would create discussion. My memoir is part of breaking down this unspoken reality and why I must stay steadfast.

I do not want my story to appear more ugly than it really was. A big concern for me in revealing details about my life is to show that familial sexual abuse occurs not only in what can be viewed as obviously dysfunctional families, but in apparently acceptable family situations, such as with nice people. Not that I am suggesting our family was of this milieu. On the surface, my family was of the usual type. There were good times and not-so-good times we shared together, there was a character, like my father, who behaved badly and a child, like me, who was shy and inward-looking. I may have been insecure, but I had heard the snow goose story. I was not destroyed by what had happened to me as a little girl. In fact, many would say life has been good to me. The same could be said for my brother.

Peggy would often say how proud she was of how her two children had grown up and what they had achieved. My mother, too, was much respected in the various communities she was part of, and I remember many of my friends looking up to her and liking her very much. One friend, who knows my story, still remembers her as a very interesting woman. It was obvious she had a different outlook on life compared to most women: her fascination with the religious made her atypical. It could also be said, she was a woman before her time.

On the outside, we appeared to be an ordinary run-of-the-mill family and a successful one at that. The apparent normalness of our family is at the crux of this account of familial sexual abuse. How easy it was, and I believe still is, to perpetuate abuse of this nature.

The reaction of horror from my cousin, who was part of our early life together – one of our holiday playmates – on hearing of the sexual abuse in our family, suggests the extent to which abuse of this sort can be concealed. This cousin saw more of my brother and me than anyone else, certainly in the first ten years of my life, yet he was completely unaware of what was happening behind the scenes he was so often involved in. I wonder if the general ignorance around familial sexual abuse is because of not only the silence but the difficulty of coming to grips with it for those who have not been subjected to this sort of abuse. Perhaps it is a step too far for some.

My remark that I did not feel as though I was a casualty of sexual abuse requires clarification – of course I was. Emotionally frozen and internally contained, I have struggled to show feelings for most of my life. Sounds like a casualty to me.

Having researched a little of the work on adult Attachment Theory, I have identified myself as close to being an 'avoidant' – someone who is uncomfortable being close to others, finds it difficult to trust completely, and is challenged when needing to depend on another. According to psychologists, this insecure attachment occurs in twenty per cent of relationships.

Other insecure styles are the 'anxious', who seek approval and support from their partners and cannot think about living alone, and the 'disorganised', who want intimacy and closeness but at the same time experience trouble trusting and depending on others. Fortunately, the dominant attachment style is the secure one, where, amongst other attributes, an individual is comfortable expressing emotion openly.

I am told it is possible to change from an insecure to secure attachment way of being and this is my hope for myself. I accept I have attachment difficulties when it comes to my relationships with men. My apparent detachment in their presence clearly stems from my relationship with my father. I now understand why the word aloof has often been used to describe me.

There are further thoughts I have had about my constantly wanting to write about my mother. Was there more than my need to comprehend her religious journey, to carry out our contract? Did a part of me deliberately want to avoid writing my own story? Unconsciously I knew of my history and recognised the agony involved in facing up to it and writing about it.

Dotted throughout the narrative about myself I have recognised how much easier it would be not to tell of the happenings in our family. Driven on by a force stronger than myself I have overcome the torment of opening up.

Peggy's observation to my brother and myself, in her journal, confirms the means she adopted to erase unpleasant facts from her mind. She wrote:

'I'm sure you both know psychological pain is created only by the mind and the secret of being free of that pain which humanity suffers from, is just to be aware in the presence of each moment.'

Did you really think it was so easy, my dear mother?

I have wondered if Peggy's constant search for the silent mind became a very convenient distraction for her. She could almost believe this was what her life was about. It certainly would have helped her avoid accepting responsibility for any harm done to her children. The often-used comment during the last years of her life, 'I've had a good life,' evokes a positive assurance about herself. That look of sadness a few months before she died suggests otherwise.

For myself, there is now optimism and hope. The word contentment is not one usually associated with my way of functioning in the world, yet I notice a serenity has entered my life. I am much quieter within myself. My thoughts are much less troubled, more uncomplicated, and less obtrusive. Although I spend a lot of time alone, I am content with what my life has become. Perhaps it is the innate writer settling more comfortably within me. Having just read an article on the Modern Elder Academy there is a realisation I can call myself a modern elder; someone who in the later stage of life has a contribution to make to society. The future is looking bright.

Helping me maintain this positive outlook is the ongoing relationship I have with the birds who fly into my property. They hold my attention on a constant basis. There are no bowerbirds or seagulls, but many others. Whether it is the noisy cockatoos, the flashy lorikeets or the gentle nectar eaters dangling from my plants as they gather sustenance, they are all part of my life now. So too are the kookaburras with their magical laughter. What joy as I observed two of them bathing in my big bird bath yesterday.

Over the last few weeks, I have been watching a currawong gathering material for the building of her nest, which she now sits on, high above the ground on an outer branch of one of my old rainforest trees. She looks to be so precarious but has sat there, through rain and wind, for almost three weeks now. Perhaps I can learn from her steadfastness.

The impact from hearing the story about the snow goose as a young child clearly remains with me today, as seen in my attention to these birds. The snow goose showed my child self that it was possible to heal and fly away. Today the story still provides me with the inspiration to fly high and let go. My goal is to be free from all that has restricted my life.

Reminding me of this aspiration is a quote from Jung, which I have written out and attached to the side of my computer; 'I am not what happened to me, I am what I choose to become.' Every time I sit at my computer these words, in big red letters, challenge me to do what I have promised myself to carry out. The ingrained desire to resist opening up and stay private and closed is strong. So too is the urge to make public the trauma and experience of my life in the hope that others who have experienced childhood sexual abuse may be helped.

One of the more significant experiences for me in recent months is the help I have received from a psychologist. This woman has helped me understand what was happening for me emotionally both during my life and this last decade as I continued to write. Being able to attribute some psychological intelligence to my emotional backwardness has clarified issues and opened whole new ways in which I have been able to view my history. Those voiceless thoughts are a thing of the past.

More than this, in the last few days I have been able to unlock and reprocess information on the trauma that has held me captive for so long. The psychologist has taken me through a session of EMDR (Eye Movement Desensitization and Reprocessing) and the effect of undergoing this procedure has left me almost speechless and certainly grateful. The fact that I have gone through only one session, and can notice such a difference in my outlook, is mind-blowing.

EMDR is based on the idea that some traumatic events are not properly processed in the brain when they happen. If this occurs it is possible that long after the event, triggers can disturb and stress those, like myself, who have been left traumatised. A relatively recent addition to psychology, it was in 1987 when psychologist Francine Shapiro was walking through a park thinking about some painful memories when she noticed that rapid eye movements reduced the distress she was feeling. What was significant here, was the side-to-side eye movements which involve both sides of the brain. At first sceptical, she exposed her observation to years of experimentation and eventually created a standardised procedure to take those disturbed in this way back to the trauma and reprocess it.

In my case the psychologist arranged our seating at an angle and used a stick, slowly moving it from side to side as I followed with my eyes while taking the occasional deep breath. Every few moments she would stop and ask me how I felt and told me to pay attention to this feeling or the memory the feeling came from. Deep breath and then stop and notice the feeling. And so it carried on.

It was the bedroom scene on a Sunday morning which seemed to hold some horror for me, and which the psychologist took me back to for this session. The distress I felt when thinking of this scene was something I was unable to rid myself of. I could not put words to the feeling. It was almost as though my head, or was it my brain, could not comprehend.

When I returned to this scene during the process of EMDR I was able to find out the extent of what happened. Under the influence of EMDR, I saw the scene as I have previously described it. For example, there was the distinct image of the bed and our family in it, and there was the moment my mother turned her back on what was occurring. What was new to me was that I fled from the bed, and my father and my little brother went silent. Previously, I had no recall of taking flight. This part of the scene was blocked by the trauma of what my little girl self was experiencing with my father on those Sundays. It was the sexual abuse I remembered, not the part where I saved myself from probably a deeper, further harm. I was able to escape.

These images, on first remembering them left me feeling, 'was that all?' How could my life be ruled by this experience? How could this dictate how I interacted with people, particularly those of the male species?

Bessel van der Kolk, one of the world's experts on traumatic stress, has explained exactly how I was affected a few days ago. EMDR, he writes, seems to help 'put the traumatic experience into a larger context or perspective'. My feeling now is one of relief. I do not need to revisit that scene – and dare I say, it is over.

On reflection, I think there was much more going on in these images than first appearances suggest. My mother turning away indicates something unusual was happening. And what was I running from? Did my little girl self instinctively understand I was under threat?

A possible explanation can be found if I reframe this picture. I feel my father was about to take his touching of my little body a step further than had previously happened on these Sunday mornings. His body gave him away, my mother saw and turned her gaze, while I jumped off the bed with a sense of unease. The silence from my little brother was possibly a reaction to the sudden change in the scene unfolding.

These deliberations I see as only that – possible musings and considerations. But I do wonder if I had been able to recall my escape from that bed, whether the distress associated with the bedroom scene would have stayed with me. How would my life have played out?

The knowledge I could make myself safe seems a powerful one for a little girl to take on. If I had remembered, perhaps anxiety would not have played such a big part in my life. And most importantly, it is feasible that the lifelong habit of freezing out emotions to keep myself safe may not have developed. It has been explained to me that if I had received counselling from my mother at this time, my life could have been so different. Instead, I grew up with a memory fragment. Google explains: During a traumatic experience, memories can be encoded irregularly which creates imperfections in the memory.

For now, I am thankful for the experience of EMDR and how it has left me – free, and like the snow goose, able to fly high. That little knot in my inner being – that thing which has unconsciously dictated how I operated in the world – has been dispersed. Perhaps the flutter in my heart will now begin to melt away.

On Memory

In a final search for understanding, I have decided to investigate how we remember from a scientific basis. All my ruminations about soul contracts, weird happenings, and intuitive understanding may make sense to me and help explain who I have become. However, for others, a more scientific approach to memory could be necessary to comprehend and accept the way this story has unfolded. In great anticipation, I am once more going to put on my research hat and investigate memory and its environs. Questions such as: How trustworthy are memories? Can memory be distorted? What does it mean to have a memory of a particular event? Why does one memory arise over and above another? Whether I can find answers to these questions remains to be seen.

After a few days of limited research, I have discovered some interesting facts about how we remember. I have learnt that my tapping of the knees has been likened to EMDR. The slow alternative tapping of my knees from left to right is akin to the left-right eye movements I did with the psychologist. So too, EFT (Emotional Freedom Technique) tapping, a tool used in psychology to relieve anxiety and depression, is similar. My procedure is not as unconventional as I thought. This is quite heartening for me – I am not so different and out there after all. And of course, I now realise the man who taught me to tap was a grief counsellor who no doubt had extensive training in psychology. How fortunate I was able to learn this technique. It has been central to unravelling those parts of my life which I preferred to forget, for so very long.

A walk through, an exploration of the main parts of the brain involved in memory, helps to explain how the brain develops during our early years. It is a relief for me to have learnt that those various moments of remembering the difficult times in my early life coincide with the progress of my brain as a child. It is in the hippocampus we hold memories of events that happened to us. These are episodic or explicit memories. Or those we can consciously recall and discuss, such as my memories of sexual abuse. Implicit memories are unconscious and automatic and are those we do every day, for instance when the young learn how to ride a bike or learn to swim. When we are born, we do not have a hippocampus, but from the age of around two years, it reaches some degree of maturity and is almost fully formed by the age of five to seven.

Close to the hippocampus is the amygdala which regulates emotion and is where the 'fight or flight' response comes from. The psychiatrist, Professor Veronica O'Keane, has described the amygdala as the 'emotional spark plug'. In females, it becomes highly developed around the age of four with only small increases in development in later years. My amygdala would have been fully utilised as my five-year-old self ran away from that bed and my father. These two areas of the brain are significant to my story and the issue of memory; however, it should be noted the brain itself does not reach full maturity until twenty-five years of age.

The question of infantile amnesia, sometimes called childhood amnesia, is significant for understanding my recollections. Numerous theories are produced for why the very normal circumstance of forgetting early memories occurs. This is concerned with the inability of adults to remember events from early infancy, after the age of two and up to at least six years old. An important consideration is obviously that the brain, and particularly its memory parts, are still maturing when we are young.

Recent research on rats has shown that despite the apparent loss of early episodic memories, a trace of the memory of an early experience remains for a long period of time and can be triggered by a later reminder. However, the more emotion there is in a memory the more likely it is to survive childhood amnesia. Perhaps this is why the two big emotional experiences in my early life, the touching scene and the bedroom scene, have eventually been remembered. The American neurosurgeon, Jon T. Willie, has explained, 'If you have an emotional experience the amygdala seems to tag that memory in such a way it is better remembered.'

Also noteworthy is the Freudian theory that 'driven by motives we do not understand we are not in control of our own behaviour'. This idea still holds, although today there is scientific evidence which has shown us how our conduct creates neural pathways which are formed in the brain. It is now not just theory. Neural pathways are the connections formed between neurons in the brain (brain cells). Every thought we have, whether it is about love or an orange, is a neural pathway. Every feeling or action has a neural pathway. Like pathways generally, the more we tread over a neural pathway the more we get to know it. The basis of all our habits originates from a neural pathway. In this way, the safety mechanism I developed of shutting down and walking away whenever an emotional threat crossed my path was perpetuated and deepened. It became my little habit. No, more than that, it was almost an addiction. Freeze and I could handle any emotional disturbance. It is interesting for me to note that the word freeze has been added to descriptions of the fight or flight response humans can experience when under threat.

Then there is the debate about repressed memory or false memory. Recently this question has emerged in sexual abuse cases that have come before the courts in Australia. The American clinical psychologist, Richard McNally has stated:

> 'The notion that traumatic events can be repressed and later recovered is the most pernicious bit of folklore ever to infect psychology and psychiatry. It has provided the theoretical basis for 'recovered memory therapy' – the worst catastrophe to befall the mental health field since the lobotomy era.'

Strong words indeed. I wonder where he would place my experience. Hinted at by both my mother and my cousin, the memory of being sexually abused at the hands of my father was repressed by me for many years. Perhaps McNally would prefer to call my memories false memory? If so, I wonder on what basis he would argue for this.

Further readings suggest the re-emergence of memories usually means that the previous emotional hurt was repressed because the individual was not in a safe or stable enough place to heal.

I believe I put the trauma of sexual abuse into a 'deep freeze' so I could function in day-to-day life. This is how I coped as a child and later as an adult. Moreover, the involvement of my mother in exposing the abuse suggests repression is a valid position. Although Peggy may have prevaricated on the issue, it is impossible to see her as an innocent bystander. She was very much part of the disclosure.

***

This is as far as I got with my writing of this segment on memory when I had a minor stroke. It may have been only a little stroke, but how monumental this experience has been for me.

What it has shown me is how our journeys of self-discovery can carry on in the most unexpected ways. We may think we have reached the heart of the matter and then something else occurs. More comes to the surface and another layer of the onion is peeled away. Not in my wildest imagination could I have envisioned this happening to me. I am a very fit and healthy-looking woman in my 70s and have carried this hale and hearty persona alongside me all my life, so it seems. Over the last few weeks whenever I have told someone, who knows me, about my having had a stroke, they look at me in disbelief. Yet I now understand that what happened is purely a continuation of my history.

A session with the psychologist was the setting for this next learning experience. She was explaining to me how engaging with an emotional situation was more beneficial than walking away from it.

For example, whenever my husband Jamie produced one of his verbal assaults on me, if only I had sat down with him and at least tried to talk it through. What was happening and why? Could we overcome these abusive occasions? Our life together could have been so much easier. But no, through the practice and repetition of walking away, I formed a neural pathway which became a habit in the way I interacted with Jamie.

The emotional circumstance the psychologist chose to expand on was that between Leon and myself. This is the latest relationship I had with a man. We had so enjoyed ourselves in London. Was it simply a good time with a bit of sex thrown in? Or perhaps we could meet up again and develop our friendship? As she explained how I could have talked through the situation with him, I felt myself internally saying, *No, no, I can't do that, no, no.* My brain was hardwired to walk away from emotional discussions. I could not see myself changing. Hence my little stroke of luck. I am sure it happened while I was deep into saying *no, no,* to myself.

What also occurred for me in these few moments was the full comprehension of how I had lived my whole life evading anything that could develop into an emotional encounter. Previously I had acknowledged this tendency but not really and truly admitted to it. As the psychologist verbalised how I could help myself, I had no feeling of being overwhelmed. There was no agitation. It was simply, *no, no.* I absolutely understood what she was suggesting, and there was nothing to indicate what was about to happen.

Once the session with the psychologist ended and I stood up, my left leg did not want to accompany me. The leg from the knee down felt weak and gave the impression of giving way under me. I seemed to trip out of the psychologist's doorway and when I reached the front door of the office, I appeared to trip again. As I walked to my car the tripping continued. *Funny,* I thought.

I drove home – down the highway and up the winding mountain road. Once I reached the top of the mountain, I could see the car seemed to be veering to the left towards the driveways on the edge of the road. *Funny,* I thought.

I called in to see a girlfriend and tripped into her house. She observed I looked rather grey. Perhaps something to eat and drink would help.

As I drove away, turning to the left away from my friend's house, I thought, *This is difficult, I am not seeing the road properly. Is the sun too strong for my eyes?* Once home, I rested and thought, *This will all go away just as it did in Hobart.*

I now realise the experience I had in Hobart with weak legs and a sweaty body was a little warning. Again, it was an emotional experience. It was in Hobart, when I finally accepted my father's definite intention to abuse me, that my body went into an emotional panic.

On waking at home the next morning, I could see my tripping was more than a casual occurrence. There was no change, I was still tripping. During the night I had wondered about the possibility of my having had a stroke. Hospital seemed the safest place to be, so I rang for an ambulance.

I was told the MRI taken in the hospital had identified a TIA (transient ischaemic attack) previously and this probably happened during the Hobart incident. After various scans, it was revealed the limbic system, which deals with emotions and memory, was affected. Of course it was. Unbeknown to me, while I sat listening to 'advice' from the psychologist, I simply had a rather large and internal emotional meltdown. The emotional centre of my brain which includes the hippocampus and amygdala went into threatened mode. In fact, I can imagine it almost collapsed at the thought of having an emotional discussion with Leon.

When I examine my book on the language of the body, I see having a stroke can indicate the inability to change. Oh dear, oh dear. How I have set myself up for exactly this situation.

At the hospital, I was put on a very high dose of statins which sent me into an emotional freefall. Depression began to accompany me during these weeks. The fact of my having had a stroke probably did nothing to help my negative state of mind. How could this happen to me?

Now I am on a much lower dose of these pills, my joy for life has returned and I have started to write again. The most important thing I have learnt from this experience is that I am not invincible, and I need to tread more carefully and be more mindful of my emotional health. That there is a certain fragility around my emotional well-being is obvious but what is also clear is that I cannot continue to control my emotional responses by closing down. I must open myself to emotional dialogue if and when the occasion presents itself.

I have been very lucky because there is very little permanent damage to my body, if any. The statistics suggest only ten per cent of people fully recover from a stroke. I must confess to a certain feeling of weakness in both legs when I stand, although it has been explained to me this is probably because of the trauma my body has experienced. Time and exercise will strengthen my legs. The physiotherapist has identified a weakness in the toes of my left foot. I have exercises to make my toes stronger and I ensure a very definite neural pathway for walking is being generated by occasionally stamping my way to the local shop to buy the morning newspaper.

When the stroke first happened, I grabbed a walking stick to help steady myself. Bought in Paris at a time when one of my hips was in trouble, I took it to the hospital with me. However, I had already done my research on neural pathways and understood about creating positive pathways in the brain. Establishing a pathway which consisted of walking with a stick was not something to be encouraged. My Parisian walking stick is back in my study.

Having had a stroke has introduced me to many appointments with medical doctors. Discussions about my health with the medical profession are something I have avoided for most of my life. My preference has always been to go down the 'alternative' route. Natural therapies such as those practised by naturopaths, acupuncturists and kinesiologists have always been my preferred course of action. I have never thought about why I favoured this path over the established institutional practice of medicine.

The local doctor I have recently started to spend time with and who I have developed an enormous respect for has identified a significant factor in the make-up of my personality. This doctor knows of my history and my inclination towards natural therapies. She told me of an article she had recently read about children of sexual abuse and how they avoid relationships with authority figures, such as those in the medical profession.

Lack of trust was the basis for this conduct. A light bulb went off in my head as she explained. Some of those decisions and events from my life which I have struggled to understand were suddenly made clear.

One time I have always wondered about was the period I spent studying at university. For nearly ten years I was a mature-age student. Outwardly I was a confident and very together woman in my forties, but as a student, I became shy and inward-looking. Indeed, when I did not receive the first-class honours for my Bachelor of Arts that I thought I was entitled to, I was distraught (first-class honours were required to automatically carry on towards study for a PhD) but I did not confront the department head. I seemed frozen and unable to speak up for myself. Instead, one of my university lecturers, who had recently arrived back from an overseas trip, spoke for me, with the result that I went straight into the PhD programme.

At the time I did not understand why I was unable to challenge the authority of the university system. Now I know why. Further, the inhibition which was part of my everyday life during my time at university is now made clear to me. University teachers, like the medical profession, are figures of authority. Just like fathers.

What has been another big lesson for me is I have learnt I am not alone in this world. Something I could never have envisioned was that I was unable to drive for a whole month after the stroke. When the hospital doctor told me I was not allowed to drive, my immediate response was true to character, "Well, you know I will drive." I promptly got the sort of telling-off that ensured I left my car in the garage for the required four weeks. During this time, a variety of friends and neighbours drove me around. Almost every day there was somewhere I was required to be, and with no public transport on the mountain, there was always someone who was there for me. This was an enormous learning curve for me. One of my friends called these outings 'driving Miss Daisy'. I jotted in my journal three weeks into being home:

> 'Have learnt am not a lone island – cannot be in this world – and this really is not acceptable. We are here to be with others and learn to relate to them. I have a lot to learn regarding this. So much easier to be alone ... there is more joy in sharing and doing with others. Fancy having to learn these things at my age. Have I been slow – too slow? No, think I had to learn about other things before this next learning. Oh my, oh my.'

The realisation of how kind and loving people can be, has been like an enormous gift to me.

The question must be asked: Did the psychologist push me too far? Perhaps! She did know that Leon had been a weak spot for me, but it was not so much the issue of Leon, as my inability to change my emotional responses which sent me into a negative spin which ended in a stroke. She could not have known how deeply entrenched the mindset to freeze was in my brain. Nor could she have known how unshakeable my desire was to avoid emotional discussions. Perhaps she had not delved deep enough. However, I have called this experience my 'stroke of luck' because I have a sense that without the stroke, I might never have known how emotionally backward I am and have been throughout my life. Perhaps I would have continued squashing this vulnerability to my much deeper detriment. I have been given a chance to mend my ways. The plasticity of the brain means we can change habits and create new neural pathways and even dissolve old ones. Again, how lucky I am that the psychologist triggered me to the extent she did. She was the catalyst for my learning, and I am very grateful.

For the moment, I am resting in the knowledge of my emotional shortcomings and have the full intention of educating myself back to emotional health. Part of the route to mending my inadequacies has been in the writing of this memoir. It seems so long ago that I started to write about my life. When I began, it was with the intention of bringing to light the way familial sexual abuse can occur so easily – and how effortlessly it can remain hidden within the family. So much more has been revealed. If nothing else has been learnt but that wherever there is sexual abuse it leaves its mark, then my writing has been worthwhile. I have taken heed of the words from the Danish philosopher, Soren Kierkegaard who wrote, 'Life can only be understood backward but it must be lived forward.' I now have that understanding about my life and the objective from now on is simply to accept and welcome what comes into my everyday life.

Meanwhile, I continue to be enthralled by the birds flying into and through my rainforest trees. The snow goose story remains fundamental to my well-being as seen in my concentration on these birds.

My attention for the moment has been caught by a currawong flitting from tree to tree looking for little branches to break off with its beak. It is another year, and another nest is being built in the trees outside my windows.

What has also happened this year, is my large grass tree, or *Xanthorrhoea australis*, has put out eight spear-like spikes, all of which are covered with small cream flowers. This has drawn the king parrots to feed on the nectar. As they dangle upside down on the spikes, squawking and screeching with excitement, I am in awe of how beautiful and special this scene is. How lucky am I?

www.ingramcontent.com/pod-product-compliance
Lightning Source LLC
Chambersburg PA
CBHW011148290426
44109CB00024B/2535